22.00

Taking Care of Business

Taking Care of Business

How to Become More Efficient and Effective Using ISO 9000

Greg Hutchins

omneo

AN IMPRINT OF OLIVER WIGHT PUBLICATIONS, INC.

85 Allen Martin Drive
Essex Junction, VT 05452

ACKNOWLEDGMENTS

When I was looking for "killer" quotes for this book, many suggested quotes such as "ISO is the hottest thing since canned beer or sliced bread." Yawn. Boring. Unusable.

However, I am grateful to those of you who spent the time thinking through the ISO process and supplying me with your insights. You made this book a much better product.

To the following go a special thanks for your time and insightful contributions:

Nancy Araway, Quality Management Program Manager, Data General

David Ballard, Quality Consultant

Andrew Bergman, Certification Manager, OTS Quality Registrars

Jim Childs, Publisher, Oliver Wight Publications

Julie Craig, ISO Audit Manager, Data General

Karen Davis, Quality and Integration Program Manager, Data General

Emily Konold, QA Specialist, Help/Systems

Beth Krenzer, Manager, Black & White Film Manufacturing, Eastman Kodak

Karen Lovecchio, ISO 9000 Coordinator, Kodak Park Division, Eastman Kodak

Joanne Mayo, Corporate ISO Coordinator, Data General

Darryl Parker, Director, A.G.A. Quality

Debbie Peck, Publicity Manager, Oliver Wight Publications
Les Schnoll, ISO 9000 Manager, Dow Corning
Norm Seifert, Quality Consultant
Jennifer Smith, Marketing Manager, Oliver Wight Publications
John Zavacki, QA Manager, Suckle Corp.

CONTENTS

PREFACE

The title of this book, *Taking Care of Business*, was chosen because increasingly businesses are focusing on internal operations, systems, and processes to improve the bottom line. In this constrained economy, all elements of an organization's competitiveness are being examined and improved.

Traditionally, the external elements of marketing and selling often received the lion's share of your attention. The customer was king. The first product on the market or the one with the highest quality often won over customers. As long as there was high customer demand and only a small number of companies could satisfy the demand, profits were guaranteed. Now times have changed. Most companies compete and excel using similar mechanisms and processes. The critical issue is to discover and develop new ways of staying competitive, and to provide the customer value through high-quality products and services at a low cost.

The critical question for you and many others is "How do you provide value at a low cost?" The answer is to tighten up and improve internal operations. More top-management focus is being centered internally, where it can focus on what can be done to enhance productivity, to produce and deliver more with the existing or fewer resources. This is one of the major reasons for the attention and growth in ISO 9000 and the rationale for the title of this book. ISO 9000 encourages the development of organizational operational systems and processes that improve internal operations.

In the last decade, U.S. industries have lost international and domestic market share to foreign competitors in consumer electronics, steel, autos, and a host of other commodities. Basic assumptions on how to run a business have been challenged. Many solutions have been offered. The only enduring solution that has been proposed, Total Quality Management (TQM), is still around and widely used, and ISO 9000 represents the most accessible, understandable, and accepted structure for TQM.

OUR OBJECTIVE

Quite frankly, ISO 9001/9002/9003 standards are boring to read. They are technical quality standards, full of breathtaking requirements such as "Organizational and technical interfaces between different groups shall be identified and the necessary information documented, transmitted, and regularly reviewed."[1] This dense information does not lend itself to easy implementation.

Taking Care of Business goes beyond the rigorous details of the quality standards to address the broader issues of good business. If you read beyond the dense quality requirements and specifications of the ISO standards, you'll see that there are a set of commonsense business values, directions, techniques, and ideas inherent in the standards that are valuable for all businesses.

In this book, we've attempted to look at how the requirements can be used by you, the reader, in your attempts to create a better business. *Better* can be defined as operating more efficiently, providing better customer service, or producing defect-free products.

The ISO standards offer generally accepted and approved methods for operating a business. While the emphasis and examples of *Taking Care of Business* are particularly manufacturing oriented, they can be used by almost any type of organization, be it a small metal fabricator, a hospital, even a school. The standards are based on simple and sound business principles, systems, and processes. Each business and organization is structured in terms of similar and common systems that produce different products.

The products may be a pencil, happy customers, or educated students. The overlying systems in ISO 9000 are common to each operation.

ORGANIZATION OF THE BOOK

The first part of this book describes the strategic benefits of using ISO 9000 to "take care of business." Three broad categories of benefits are accrued-customer/marketing, and internal and customer-supplier partnering benefits.

The first part of this book follows a simple outline:

- *Taking Care of Business.* Chapter 1 is an overview of the critical benefits of implementing ISO 9000.

- *What Are the ISO 9000 Standards?* Chapter 2 explains the structure, purpose, and objectives of ISO 9000.

- *Customer/Marketing Benefits.* Chapter 3 describes the customer and marketing benefits of implementing ISO 9000.

- *Internal Benefits.* Chapter 4 describes the internal—organizational and operational—benefits of implementing ISO 9000.

- *Customer-Supplier Benefits.* Chapter 5 describes the supplier-benefits of implementing ISO 9000.

- *Getting Started.* Chapter 6 describes how to get started implementing and registering to ISO 9000.

The second part of this book emphasizes the "what is" and "how to" implement the 20 quality system elements of ISO 9001. The 20 quality system requirements of ISO 9001 are:

4.1 Management Responsibility

4.2 Quality Systems

PART I

An Introduction to ISO 9000

CHAPTER

1

Taking Care of Business

Business assumptions are being rethought in all organizations. Restructuring may mean downsizing, partnering, reengineering, or outsourcing. Companies have discovered that the old ways of doing business don't necessarily work anymore and that new approaches are required. The goal of these approaches is to become world class and to have the best quality, service, and delivery systems.

A major element of the restructuring effort is to use quality standards such as ISO 9000 both externally and internally. Externally, companies are adopting new systems of management, such as ISO 9000, as a means to enter new markets or to satisfy international customers. They are also using ISO 9000 as a way to link up with companies in order to develop, manufacture, and deliver products and services quickly. Internally, companies are using ISO 9000 to understand, monitor, and improve their fundamental systems and processes.

The critical question, then, becomes: How can ISO 9000 help you to "take care of your business"? The complete list of benefits is covered in the first half of this book but the following are among the most important:

- Involves top management in operations.

- Proceduralizes operations.

- Facilitates operational control.

- Encourages management by exception.

- Encourages customer-supplier partnering.

INVOLVES TOP MANAGEMENT IN OPERATIONS

A revolution has erupted in corporate America. The old ways of doing business have been tossed aside and new ways are taking over. Those who spout, "If it ain't broke, don't fix it" are corporate dinosaurs. The new spirit is "If it ain't improved, then we won't have to worry about being around to fix it."

Traditionally, organizations have been set up in departments divided into functional or professional areas. Each organizational unit developed its mandate and defended itself from intruders. Protection, inertia, conformity, and risk-averse behaviors prevailed in these organizational silos. Departments played games such as stealing ideas from other departments; avoiding ideas not invented in one's department; shooting down requests or ideas that do not conform to prevailing attitudes; guarding information that may help the overall organization; and building bureaucracies that hold people to unrealistic rules and regulations. Issues critical to competitiveness and survival were forgotten as the issues of turf and protection took over. Departmental turf wars, political posturing, or insider games are being replaced by a cooperative, team-oriented, and partnering spirit.[1]

The changes can be seen in the following areas:

- Top management is actively involved in the quality vision.

- Organizational culture, values, and ethics are changing to reflect the new quality environment.

- Quality strategy is aligned with the organization's business strategy.

- Policies, procedures, and operational instructions are vertically and horizontally aligned and harmonized with the quality business strategy.

PROCEDURALIZES OPERATIONS

By adopting ISO 9000, each process step from designing to delivering a product is done correctly the first time. If a nonconformance should arise, the monitoring and correcting quality systems will catch and correct the deficiency. For example, internal auditing is a quality system used to ensure that processes are periodically monitored. Corrective action quality systems eliminate system deficiencies.

Quality process and systems thinking complements the goals of reengineering. Proceduralization ensures that processes are smooth, continuous, and uninterrupted. Design development and other projects are performed simultaneously. And highest value is added when interruptions are minimized and proceduralized.

Proceduralization also implies that a company is willing to spend the time and effort necessary to analyze work operations and ask additional tough questions. Policies, procedures, and work instructions are analyzed. Quality systems and processes are made flexible to satisfy changing market demands.

FACILITATES OPERATIONAL CONTROL

Fundamental to ISO 9001/9002/9003 is the concept of control. What is control? Webster defines *control* as: "to check or verify; to regulate; to verify by comparison with a standard; and to exercise authority over." The last element, "to exercise authority over," is what many people object to, especially if control is being exercised over them. In the workplace, this often implies that management or a supervisor is looking over one's shoulder, telling the person how and when to do something. This is disempowering.

With the extreme downsizing and flattening of organizations taking place today, the concept of control has changed. Control is not used anymore in the authoritarian sense of controlling people but rather in having people control their operations. Control means defining standards of operation, keeping processes at the defined target, and controlling variation around the target. The goal implicit in ISO 9000 is to empower employees to control processes, to take responsibility for their area of operations, and to have the authority to change processes if necessary.

The fundamental goal of establishing and maintaining quality systems is to guarantee consistency. This is the basic principle behind monitoring and controlling processes. While these principles have their major application in manufacturing, they apply to all business operations, systems, and processes.

Consistency Is the Ability to Control Variation

Quality is the ability to develop consistent operations. Consistent or uniform products are obtained through controlling variation. The rationale for controlling variation is as follows:

- *Quality is conformance to requirements.* Customer requirements are spelled out in specifications, engineering prints, contracts, standards, and other documents. On a production line, conformance to a specification is assured by identifying a product's critical quality characteristics, monitoring them, and comparing them against the specification target. If there is any abnormal deviation, then the process producing the part is adjusted back to the nominal dimension.

- *Products and process vary.* Some say the study of quality is the study of variation—of a process producing products, for example, or of someone answering a phone. The more variation from what is prescribed in a policy, procedure, or work instruction, the higher the possibility of a product nonconformance or an action that may displease a customer.

- *Variation in processes and products can be measured.* Variation can *always* be measured. Production variation can be the result of humidity, temperature, or other variables. Production variation may be measured by sophisticated instruments that can measure to millionths of an inch. Service variation is measured by customer surveys or through quality auditing.

- *Variation follows identifiable, consistent patterns.* Variation follows distinctive, identifiable, consistent patterns. For example, in production operation a bell-shaped frequency distribution of measurements may provide evidence that the process being monitored is running normally and there are no external causes influencing it.

- *Variation due to unusual factors causes inconsistent or unusual patterns.* Variation, or in other words unusual patterns or trends, can indicate a departure from the normal. If one monitors a process over time through auditing or process control, these patterns can indicate unusual trends, sudden process changes, or cyclical variation.

- *Variation can be monitored, detected, and controlled through documented, consistent processes.* The assumption is that if variation can be detected and controlled, then quality can be verified. Quality process and system variation can be monitored and controlled. Procedures and work instructions ensure that operations are consistent. Documentation ensures that processes are running properly, and if there is an unusual condition, then quick action corrects the deficiency. These concepts are integrated into the ISO standards and form the basis of good operational management.[2]

ENCOURAGES MANAGEMENT BY EXCEPTION

Another important principle of ISO 9000 is exception management. Once the quality system is running smoothly and controls are in place, then operating personnel can manage the quality system through a process of exception management. If quality systems operate properly, then unusual occurrences, deficiencies, or nonconforming products or activities should be minimal. If there are unusual occurrences, such as unusual variations, then these indicate that the system is out of control. It's important to catch these unusual variations before nonconforming products are produced. If nonconformances do arise, the corrective action system can detect the deficiencies, isolate them, correct the cause, and ensure that they don't recur. Also, the internal quality audit system continuously monitors the maintenance and improvement of internal operations, systems, and processes.

ENCOURAGES CUSTOMER-SUPPLIER PARTNERING

A major outgrowth of the Total Quality Management effort was that suppliers were brought closer to the customer, often called customer-supplier partnering, strategic alliances, or a number of other names. The essential point is that companies are concentrating on core competencies. All other work is sourced to "world class" suppliers. Companies are working with these suppliers to develop highly engineered products that are jointly and collaboratively created with the "world class" supplier's technical personnel.

As more products require specialized components, companies are asking, "Should we make or buy the component?" The "make or buy" decision becomes a financial one where companies ask, "Do we have the expertise to manufacture a quality product at a competitive price?" Since some industrial tasks cannot be effectively accomplished in-house because of lack of equipment, trained personnel, or material, the answer to the question is often "no." What makes it an especially crucial question is that a large amount of purchased materials, assemblies, subassemblies, and components directly affect the quality of finished products.

In terms of total dollar amount, outside suppliers provide a significant portion of a manufacturer's product. For U.S. firms, 50 percent or more of the final price of a product is in the cost of purchased goods.[3] In Japan, it can be even higher.

More often, requirements for a customer-supplier relationship or partnership involve many elements of ISO 9000, including:

- ISO 9000 registration provides customer or quality commitment.

- Well-developed and-written specifications, purchase orders, contracts, and engineering prints.

- First step in certification process may be ISO registration.

- Complete quality standards and documentation exist.

- Quality management, assurance, and control systems are in place and operating.

- Independent third party verifies and periodically checks quality systems effectiveness.

- Delivery, shipping, handling, storage, and packaging capabilities meet customer requirements.

ISO 9000 are a family of documents. ISO 9001/9002/9003 are contractual "shall" documents. They describe quality requirements with which a company, usually a supplier, must comply. All other ISO documents are "should" recommendations for a company. Starting in the next chapter, we discuss and emphasize ISO 9001/9002/9003, the "shall" ISO documents.

CHAPTER

2

What Are the ISO 9000 Standards?

It's almost a given in international trading and business—if you don't have ISO registration, you have to be moving toward it or have something in place.[1]

COLIN PITTS, Manager of Quality
Implementation, BP Chemicals

Yes, large U.S. companies, both in products and services, are improving their quality. The number of deficiencies per U.S. vehicle has dropped from 7.3 in 1981 to 1.5 in 1991 and continues to decrease. The percent of deficiencies in steel products has dropped from 8 percent in 1982 to 1.5 percent in 1991. Likewise, quality in the service sector has increased. Federal Express has revolutionized the overnight carrier business by emphasizing measurable and accountable customer service, delivery, and guarantees. Pundits speculate that quality will continue to improve until quality levels in large U.S. companies reach parity with those of the Japanese.[2]

But what about the rest of U.S. industry, the hundreds of thousands of small companies that have paid lip service to quality but haven't fully implemented any quality processes? Lip service is giving way to the reality of the global marketplace of the 1990s. Companies that want to do business with most larger corporations need to have the rudiments of a quality initiative, as prescribed by the international series of quality standards, ISO 9000, Malcolm Baldrige National Quality Award, or Deming Prize. Most probably, any future quality initiative will be grounded and based on the ISO 9000 family of standards.

QUALITY AS A DYNAMIC CONCEPT

Quality is a dynamic concept, ever changing, ever moving into new areas. Until 1950, the concept of quality had to do mainly with the technical characteristics of a product. Quality was assured through the inspection of product characteristics. Now additional factors, such as design aesthetics, delivery, total cost, service, and environmental considerations, are examined throughout the product development cycle, product lifecycle, and even the delivery cycle.

New concepts and tools are being developed and integrated under the TQM umbrella, including reengineering, supplier partnering, and high-productivity teams. Originally, these concepts and practices evolved separately from quality, but now they are often considered TQM processes. The result is that more companies are adopting and adapting these practices in their operations and processes. There is no better way to manage a business than through implementing these TQM principles, and in many cases companies are using the ISO 9000 series of documents as the foundation for a TQM system.

Another critical change is that since the early 1980s, the dominant quality concern has been ensuring customer satisfaction. While that's still very important, more recently the focus has shifted to emphasizing internal elements of profitability, such as productivity, efficiency, and effectiveness.

QUALITY AS A BUSINESS IMPERATIVE

A problem with many quality initiatives is that they have not fully been adopted as a business imperative, particularly in small organizations. Over the years, quality has been driven by technical, organizational, marketing, and public-relations concerns, but often hasn't been a strategic requisite. This occurred because quality was defined in terms of the context, perspective, or needs of the user. If a person had a statistical background, he or she emphasized the technical elements of quality. Likewise, market-driven organizations focused on the customer. While all of these emphases were important, there was no overarching approach to quality except through the Malcolm Baldrige National Quality Award criteria, which were considered "world class," gimmicky, or unattainable by the vast majority of small U.S. companies. There needed to be a simpler, attainable quality vehicle.

While the Baldrige criteria are stretch benchmarks, ISO 9000 criteria are considered the attainable and doable criteria as a quality baseline or platform. They are simpler, more concise, and attainable by the vast majority of companies. Manufacturing companies, service organizations, federal agencies, and local government agencies are often implementing quality systems patterned after ISO 9000 quality systems criteria. How did ISO 9000 garner so much interest and adoption?

VERIFYING INCOMING QUALITY

Customers want defect-free products. There are a number of ways this can be achieved. Receiving inspection is one method to verify that a supplier's products meet customer requirements. Another method is to rely on the supplier's declarations that products meet specifications. The supplier may provide statistical evidence such as process control charts indicating that processes are being monitored. Or the customer may audit suppliers or rely on a third party to audit suppliers.

While these methods are useful, they still are costly, redundant, or involve compromises. Inspection is not prevention. Inspection is costly and usually ineffective. Self-certification relies on the customer and supplier having a long-standing relationship and is the foundation for establishing trust. Statistical process control charts are wonderful for providing evidence of a customer's quality processes, particularly in manufacturing, but they don't indicate how administrative, professional, or service quality processes and systems are performing. Finally, redundant audits of the same firms evaluating the same criteria are expensive. Is there a better way?

It would make more sense for the supplier to have its products tested or its quality systems evaluated by a third party. A third-party assessment may involve product testing and quality systems evaluation. In product testing, a laboratory tests products against customer, regulatory, industry, or other requirements. In quality systems assessment, a third party called a registrar audits the company's quality systems against a standard such as ISO 9000. For a third-party assessment to work, the laboratory or registrar must be independent and objective. The advantage of third-party evaluations is that the certified company's name is placed on a register for all customers to see. This should eliminate the need for redundant audits.

HARMONIZING QUALITY DOCUMENTS

Many companies and industries have developed industry-specific product specifications and quality standards. Company standards may become industry standards or may be elevated to national standards, depending on their widespread adoption, acceptance, and use. The automobile, medical device, petroleum and pressure vessel industries have developed product standards that have been elevated to national and, in some cases, even to international standards.

Oil and gas is a global industry. Petroleum industry suppliers provide products and services to similar customers in compliance with American Petroleum Institute (API) standards to assure product quality. The challenge is to harmonize or standardize product and quality systems compliance of suppliers in this market. Each supplier is audited to the same standards by multiple customers. This is redundant and costly. Suppliers may be located in Houston, Tashkent, or Turin. How does a customer know that quality systems are compatible?[3]

In oil and gas, the API has developed product standards for pipelines, drilling fluids, and other materials specific to the industry. Since the drilling, transmission, and distribution of oil and gas is an international industry, API standards have been adopted throughout the world. These standards confirm that products are consistently made, are interchangeable, and have the same properties. Companies producing oil and gas products must comply with these standards.

WHAT IS ISO?

ISO is the International Organization for Standardization. It is based in Switzerland and comprises more than 90 member states. Its goal is to promote the development of international standards and methods and to ensure that products comply with or conform to these standards. ISO 9000 quality system audits are but one assessment mechanism for ensuring compliance or conformance with standards or technical requirements. Conformity assessment is a broad term that encompasses different means for assessing products and includes testing, certification, inspection, quality systems registration, and laboratory accreditation.

WHAT IS ISO 9000?

ISO 9000 is a set of five universal quality system standards. These standards provide a framework for quality assurance and management to be understood and used worldwide. ISO 9000 has been generically arranged into an integrated system embracing fundamental quality management and assurance standards and principles.

ISO 9001 is a series or family of quality documents describing a systematic structure consisting of 20 quality systems for designing and producing quality products. Quality systems consist of the organizational structure, responsibilities, processes, and resources required to implement quality. The ISO 9000 quality requirements describe the structure of the quality systems but don't describe how products are produced or services delivered.

ISO 9001/9002/9003 were originally intended to be customer-supplier contractual documents. They represent agreed-upon methods for indicating assurance that customers get what they ordered. They are characterized by "shall" statements. For example, under the "Management Responsibility" quality system requirements, ISO 9001 states: "The supplier's management shall define and document its policy and objectives for and commitment to quality." The "shall" is not meant to be a "might" or "should," but is intended to convey a mandate. The rest of the quality documents in the family are characterized by "should" statements. These are recommended practices for an organization.

ISO 9000 follows a systems approach. It defines the quality system elements and the interaction necessary between the various elements of the organization. The objective is for the quality system elements to complement one another, thereby creating synergies. The effectiveness and efficiency of the entire quality system is higher than the sum of the individual system parts.

ISO 9001/9002/9003 allow for tailoring methods and procedures to fit specific process and product requirements. The only restriction is that changes have to be reflected in procedures. As such, ISO criteria are not locked in concrete. They are broad criteria that can adapt to reflect the needs of the marketplace.

The standards were written by quality professionals throughout the world and have incorporated agreed-upon quality system principles. The 20 business principles are called quality system requirements and are explained in the second part of this book. Examples of quality systems include management responsibility, document control, process control, training, and corrective action.

ISO 9000 standards form a common language for quality. Each

country designates its own ISO 9000 differently. In the United States, the ISO 9000 series is called the Q90 series. Q91 is technically equivalent to ISO 9001. Even though the standard is named differently throughout the world, a person in Japan can specify quality requirements to a U.S. supplier using the same language and concepts.

The most commonly used ISO 9000 standards, 9000/9001/ 9002/9003/9004, are generic documents. ISO 9001/9002/ 9003 prescribe models of quality. ISO 9001 is the most comprehensive model, incorporating 20 quality system elements. The structure of these three standards is shown in *Figure 2.1.*

- *ISO 9000 Quality Management and Quality Assurance Standards—Guidelines for Selection and Use* is a road map to ISO 9001/9002/9003. It introduces fundamental quality concepts and explains how to use the "shall" standards.

- *ISO 9001 Quality Systems—Model for Quality Assurance in Design/Development, Production, Installation, and Servicing* is the most comprehensive of the "shall" standards and consists of all 20 quality system elements.

- *ISO 9002 Quality Systems—Model for Quality Assurance in Production and Installation* explains the detection and correction of production and installation. The standard covers 18 quality system elements.

- *ISO 9003 Quality Systems—Model for Quality Assurance in Final Inspection and Test* addresses the detection and correction of final inspection and testing. The standard covers 12 quality system elements.

- *ISO 9004 Quality Management and Quality System Elements—Guidelines* provides guidance on how an organization can use ISO quality principles and suggestions to develop and implement a quality system. It examines each of the quality system elements and describes how they can be used to evaluate and implement ISO 9000 quality systems.

Figure 2.1
What Is ISO 9000?

ISO 9003 12 System Requirements	ISO 9002 18 System Requirements	ISO 9001 20 System Requirements
Management Responsibility .... >	.... >	
Quality System .... >	.... >	
Product Identification and................................ >	.... >	
Traceability		
Inspection and Test Status............................. >	.... >	
Inspection and Testing .... >	.... >	
Inspection, Measuring, ... >	.... >	
and Test Equipment		
Control of Nonconforming............................. >	.... >	
Products		
Handling, Storage, Packaging......................... >	.... >	
and Delivery		
Document Control... >	.... >	
Quality Records... >	.... >	
Training .... >	.... >	
Statistical Techniques .... >	.... >	
	Internal Quality Audits .... >	
	Contract Review .... >	
	Purchasing .... >	
	Process Control...................................... >	
	Purchaser Supplied Produce................ >	
	Corrective Action................................. >	
		Design Control
		Servicing

ISO 9000 Hierarchy

A three part hierarchy establishes and governs the credibility of and use of ISO 9000:

- *Recognition.* In the regulated product sectors, the U.S. government has followed the Europeans' lead by recognizing the authority of companies or laboratories to serve as accreditors.

- *Accreditation.* Accreditors certify the ability of registrars to conduct independent audits as well as develop criteria for quality system auditors.

- *Registration.* These companies conduct audits and maintain the register of companies that have passed their audits.

In the United States presently, no governmental organization appoints accreditors or registrars. The U.S. Commerce Department's National Institute of Standards and Technology (NIST) has established a National Voluntary Conformity Assessment Systems Evaluation program. Under the program, NIST administers voluntary recognition and accreditation.

WHO CERTIFIES THE CERTIFIER?

The registration process in the United States is largely self-regulating. The registrars are companies conducting audits and maintaining the register of certified companies. However, there is a need for a mechanism for ensuring the consistency of the third-party registrars as they proliferate in the United States. This was the rationale for the formation of the Registrar Accreditation Board (RAB). RAB is governed by a board of directors from industry, academia, and quality consultants, and evaluates the quality and capability of registrars. RAB assesses the registrars based on current recognized and accepted international criteria for registration bodies. RAB has also defined the requirements for becoming a quality auditor.

Other countries have established a similar vertical structure to certify the registrars. The goal is to ensure harmony in the international certification and application of ISO 9000. Accreditation in one country is then recognized by another country. Just as all registrars audit suppliers using the same document, namely ISO 9000, accreditors assess registrars using the same internationally accepted documents. Registrars can then interpret and implement ISO 9000 uniformly across the world.

ISO REGISTRATION

ISO 9000 systems registration indicates that a supplier has been certified or audited against the quality systems requirements spelled out in ISO 9001, 9002, or 9003. Quality systems certification is the same as quality systems registration. "Certification" does not mean that the supplier is delivering a quality product or meets all of the customer's requirements. Rather, it means that the supplier has the requisite quality systems in place and operating properly.

One of the major benefits of ISO 9000 registration is that time-consuming duplicative audits and incoming-product inspections are eliminated. Another benefit is that a quality management structure consisting of documented quality systems is in place.

Who are the main registrars in the United States? There are at least 40, and many more around the world. In the United States, registrars can be divided into:

- *Private companies.* Intertek, Quality System Registrars, and others are private companies that saw a market opportunity to provide registration services.

- *European registrars.* Lloyd's Registrar Quality Assurance, DNV, and TUV are, respectively, U.K., the Netherlands, and German registrars.

- *Industry-affiliated registrars.* ABS Quality Evaluation and AGAQ are, respectively, affiliated with the shipping and natural gas industries, though both also register companies outside of their industries.

- *Company-affiliated registrars.* Du Pont and AT&T have developed internal expertise in ISO implementation and subsequently become registrars.

WORLDWIDE MOVE TO REGISTRATION

The registration process is fairly straightforward. A third-party auditor, called the registrar, visits a company and conducts a compliance audit of up to 20 quality systems. The auditor confirms that the systems are in place and functioning properly. Upon passing the audit, the company is listed on a register of certified companies.

Why is quality systems registration becoming so popular? Registration is being pursued for a number of reasons, for example:

- A company producing safety- or health-related products determines that it wants to use ISO 9000 to meet specific EC requirements.

- A customer is requiring ISO registration as a condition of business.

- A company wants to enhance its marketing reputation or use registration as a positioning mechanism.

- A company knows that ISO 9000 is recognized and becoming accepted around the world as the baseline quality standard.

- A company recognizes the advantages of being listed in a register of companies that have passed the ISO test.

How are companies pursuing registration? Depending on the industry, they are registering all their operations as quickly as possible. One company, Witco Corporation, is registering all of its North American operations—43 U.S. plants—by the end of 1993 and the rest as quickly as possible.[4]

What does a company do if it has multiple similar sites? Do all have to be audited? Air Products and Chemicals registered more than 100 sites on one ISO 9002 certificate. Multisite registration was pursued because many of the sites had very similar operations, each with very few personnel.[5]

Product Testing Advantages[6]

Product testing by an independent third party is one means of providing the customer assurance of product quality. Few companies fully understand the importance of product testing. Some of its benefits include the ability to:

- Achieve product superiority.

- Continuously improve product performance and customer satisfaction.

- Monitor potential threat levels posed by competitive products, and understand their strengths and weaknesses.

- Reduce costs of product design and manufacture.

- Measure effects of aging on certain products.

- Measure effects of price, brand name, or packaging on perceived performance and quality.

- Provide guidance to product R&D staff for development of new products and refinement of old ones.

- Monitor relative quality levels from different factories, through different channels of distribution, year after year.

- Promote product user-acceptance of new products.

BALANCING RISK, ASSURANCE, AND COST

Which of the assurance methods is the best? There isn't an easy answer to this, and deciding which method to use is a matter of balancing risk, assurance, and cost levels. Let's discuss each of these factors.

Risk is the level of exposure the customer and supplier face if a product should fail. Risk may be nonexistent, negligible, or high. For example, the risk of failure for a commodity, such as a raw material, is relatively low. Even if the raw material is finished into a fastener such as a screw, the risk of failure may still be relatively small depending on its application. But while the probability of failure of a screw in a heart pacemaker may be relatively low, the consequence of failure is high. High risk requires a higher level of assurance, which costs more.

In general, assurance and risk are complementary. The risk of failure in regulated products such as medical devices, elevators, and nuclear power plants is relatively high. These products require a higher level of assurance. Conversely, low-risk products require lower levels of assurance.

Costs are closely linked to the risk/assurance tradeoff. As a rule, the higher the level of assurance, the higher the cost. All companies want high levels of assurance and low levels of risk. However, this adds costs. The challenge is to determine the level at which risks, assurance, and costs are acceptable.

What does this discussion of risk, assurance, and costs have to do with ISO 9000? Everything. The purpose of ISO 9001/9002/9003 registration is to provide the customer with assurance of a supplier's quality systems and its products. Compared to the other alternatives, self-certification or product testing, a quality system assessment provides the customer with a higher level of assurance that the supplier is capable of meeting the customer's requirements. The risk to the customer is that the supplier is incapable of providing products. However, as mentioned, higher

levels of assurance cost more than self-certification or product
testing.

Fastener Act

Product quality sometimes becomes a national issue. Federal
legislation prohibiting the sale of defective fasteners was
recently passed and became law. The problem resulted when
millions of substandard, mismarked, or counterfeit mechani-
cal fasteners flooded the market and were causing safety
problems. These substandard or defective nuts, screws, and
washers were used in applications such as nuclear power
plants and submarines, where a catastrophic failure could
cause the loss of life.[7]

The problem was that purchasers had been buying a
commodity—fasteners—primarily based on lowest price.
The purchaser would often require a product quality certification, but since fasteners were a commodity, the purchaser
did not take them seriously. These offshore certifications
were sometimes fraudulent, as the buyer realized when fasteners failed in critical use. The problem was that buyers were
not aware of the extent of the field problems outside their
industry, did not know where the fasteners originated because they were purchased from distributors, or could not
read the foreign test reports.

Buyers of fasteners are now changing their buying habits as:

- Quality becomes more important than price in the decision to buy.

- Buyers visit and audit distributors' facilities.

- Buyers are suspicious of especially low-cost fasteners.

- Accredited labs are used to test products.

- Suppliers are required to provide fastener samples and have them tested by accredited labs.

- Customers are recommending or insisting that suppliers and distributors be ISO registered.

In Chapter 3, we discuss the external benefits, specifically those related to the customer and marketing, of adopting ISO 9000 family documents.

CHAPTER 3

Customer/Marketing Benefits

A recent study of product innovation in the scientific instrument and tool machinery industries indicates that 80 percent of all production innovations are initiated by the customer.

ERIC VON HIPPEL,
management consultant

ISO registration is a worldwide phenomenon. In the late 1980s, European chemical companies became one of the first industry sectors to require suppliers to become registered. Rhone-Poulenc, an international chemical company, views ISO 9000 as a requirement of business. BP Chemicals initiated its quality drive in 1987 and by 1992 had 90 percent of its worldwide activities registered. In the United States, Du Pont was one of the first companies to actively pursue registration of its internal divisions and encourage external suppliers to pursue registration.[1] In this country and around the world, suppliers that don't care to register are already having difficulty acquiring business.

In most cases, the customer or the competition drives the ISO 9000 registration process. The customer may be a regulatory authority or the buyer—someone who buys products or services that sustain an organization and provide employment.

The second driver of registration is competition. Companies started adopting ISO 9000 as their means to distinguish themselves from the competition. Companies become registered so as not to lose business.

GROWTH OF ISO REGISTRATION FOR NONREGULATED PRODUCTS

The explosion in ISO 9000 registration is mainly coming from the commercial nonregulated industry sectors where registration is not required by the government. These customers are requiring suppliers to have extensive quality programs that are periodically audited. These customer-supplier initiatives, sometimes called qualification efforts, may assess a supplier's quality, delivery, cost, technology, and service capabilities.

Once a supplier has developed stable quality systems, the customer would audit a supplier for compliance to its requirements. Within a vertical industry sector, quality requirements among companies are often similar. The result was that multiple suppliers may audit a common supplier for compliance to this same criteria. Instead of auditing suppliers to the same criteria, it makes more sense to submit to only one audit, such as ISO 9000, and have the results accessible to all parties.

ISO 9000 quality systems implementation and registration offers the following marketing and customer advantages:

- Assists in developing products.

- Provides access to markets.

- Conveys commitment to quality and partnering.

- Fulfills contract requirements.

- Establishes promotional credibility.

- Conveys operational and systems assurance.

Assists in Developing Products

If quality systems are in place and in control, a new product can be designed and introduced into the marketplace more quickly because production has been stabilized, improvement teams are in place, and suppliers have already been selected.

Time-to-market is an important weapon for competitive success. The benefits of accelerated product development include higher margins, lower costs, and higher quality. A McKinsey & Company report concluded that products entering the market late but within budget average 33 percent less profit over a five-year period than products arriving on time and within budget. Interestingly, products completed on time but 50 percent over budget have only a 4 percent profit over five years.[2]

Provides Access to Markets

ISO 9000 registration is a nationally and internationally accepted mechanism for ensuring compatibility among regulated products. In Europe and elsewhere, governments are requesting and, in some cases, requiring that imported safety- and health-related products be registered, produced by a registered company, or product-tested by a certified third-party laboratory. Within Europe and other parts of the world, tested products may carry labels validating that they have been evaluated and meet national regulations.

ISO 9000 registration provides access to markets. Customer requirements, standards, specifications, capabilities, systems, and many other factors can be radically different across national boundaries. In the fluid movement of products, ISO 9000 registration is a way to maintain assurance so that quality systems from company to company and country to country are compatible.

Conveys Commitment to Quality and Partnering

While ISO 9000 registration does not affirm product quality, it does indicate that a company is concerned about satisfying customer requirements by demonstrating that it has developed, documented, and implemented company-wide quality systems. And, if the quality systems are in place and operating properly the output of these systems should satisfy customer requirements.

Registration requires a commitment of time, money, and other resources. Customers view this commitment as an important value-adding activity in the ongoing customer-supplier partnership.

Fulfills Contract Requirements

A line item on a contract or purchase order recommending or requiring ISO registration is becoming increasingly common. The line item may state: "ISO 9002 registration is preferred in companies bidding on the following telecommunications components . . ."

While this preference clause does not mandate ISO registration, it does establish the importance of quality and of ISO registration. Therefore, suppliers that are already registered may have a leg up on the competition. The next time a similar contract is let, the preference may become a requirement.

Establishes Promotional Credibility

Even companies that don't produce a regulated product or aren't required to register are doing so in order to enhance their market credibility. They can then tout this fact in their promotional literature, and improve their position in crowded markets or in industries where they may be the first company to have become registered.

Conveys Operational and Systems Assurance

ISO registration informs the customer that the supplier's internal quality systems have been audited by an independent third party. This party has established auditing procedures to determine that the supplier has the requisite quality systems. While registration

EXPERT'S CORNER
Insights and Tips

Eastman Kodak's Black and White Film Manufacturing has received customer inquiries in health sciences, printing, and publishing regarding ISO 9002 registration. Once we registered, we found that many customers wanted a copy of our quality manual and wanted to display our ISO 9002 certificate.

Our customers display our ISO registration certificate in their lobbies to assure their customers that they are dealing with quality suppliers. We also found that our customers are pursuing their own ISO 9000/9002 registrations and they were excited that Black-and-White film was registered. We found it is much easier to work with registered suppliers. Our customers have seen improved quality products, and this is reflected in fewer customer complaints.

> BETH KRENZER, Manager, Black and
> White Film Manufacturing,
> Eastman Kodak

Being ISO registered informs customers that Data General has an effective quality system in place. This eliminates the need for customers to perform source inspections at facilities. Although most customers at present are not requiring ISO registration, often a company will select an ISO-compliant supplier rather than one that is not. The combination of Data General's superior product-service offerings and ISO registration is winning the confidence of customers worldwide.

In conclusion, an effective quality system reduces costs and establishes the framework for continual quality-enhancement programs, thus leading to satisfied customers. At Data General, quality is when the customer returns and the product doesn't.

> JOANNE MAYO, Corporate ISO
> Coordinator, Data General

indicates the existence of quality systems, it does not indicate that products are quality-made or satisfy customer requirements. The quip sometimes heard that "a company can be registered to ISO 9001 and still produce nonconforming products" is very true.

However, quality systems registration is an assurance mechanism. While risks may still exist, they are appreciably lower than if the supplier had no quality systems or operational controls. In some cases, risk may still exist because the supplier doesn't follow the procedures all the time.

In Chapter 4, we discuss the internal benefits of implementing ISO 9000.

4

Internal Benefits

[Manufacturing] excellence results from dedication to daily progress. Making something a little better every day.
ROBERT HALL, educator

MULTIPLE INTERNAL BENEFITS OF ISO

ISO implementation and registration offers internal benefits that will make your operations more efficient and effective. Specifically, ISO implementation offers the following benefits:

- Guarantees that new and existing products and services satisfy customers.

- Facilitates business and quality planning.

- Provides a universal approach to quality.

- Can be used in many industries.

- Assists in establishing operational baselines.

- Operationalizes quality.

- Provides insights on organizational interrelationships.

- Encourages an internal focus.

- Facilitates internal operational control.

- Assists employees in understanding and improving operations.

- Encourages self-assessment.

- Maintains internal consistency.

- Controls processes and systems.

- Establishes operational controls.

- Makes internal operations more efficient and effective.

- Ensures that product design changes are controlled.

- Creates awareness of the need for training.

- Encourages operational problem solving.

Guarantees that New and Existing Products and Services Satisfy Customers

Rapid product development, which brings multidisciplinary teams together to develop marketable products, is a requisite for survival in the competitive marketplace. However, many people and teams working together against deadlines can be the source of miscommunication, deficiencies, rework, blind alleys, and many other complications.

ISO 9000 provides a structured process, consistent language, and common goal in this intense product development process. The cost of changes late in the development cycle or while in the hands of the customer increases exponentially. For example, a product recall or a class action litigation is much more expensive than correcting a calculation error discovered during design review.

Moreover, if a process or product has to be modified, then the ISO-structured process of reviewing designs, controlling processes, and correcting problems minimizes risks following product release. Why? ISO 9000 requires that the following quality systems are in place: Designs are thoroughly reviewed. Processes are controlled. Purchased materials are monitored. Work instructions convey quality requirements at each critical work station. Departments review and sign off on the product.

Facilitates Business and Quality Planning

The quality plan identifies customers' quality requirements and the resources needed to initiate and complete a project without rework or deficiencies. Quality is checked, monitored, and, if required, corrected at each step of developing and delivering a product.

Quality planning involves developing the appropriate quality strategies and tactics for implementing quality systems and processes. Quality planning becomes a fundamental element of any business process. At a minimum, it involves:

- Understanding customer requirements and expectations.

- Defining the project scope and objectives.

- Obtaining sufficient resources to complete the project.

- Reviewing and modifying the plan to satisfy customers' requirements.

- Securing sufficient resources to finish the project.

- Initiating the project.[1]

Provides a Universal Approach to Quality

There are multiple definitions and perspectives of TQM. ISO 9000 provides an accepted and universal approach to Total Quality Management by:

- Harmonizing different customer-supplier quality certifications schemes.

- Establishing common definitions for quality concepts and terms.

- Establishing defined series of quality system controls.

- Providing a universal platform or foundation for a quality initiative.

Can Be Used in Many Industries

ISO 9000 is a family of documents that are basically "one size fits all." They are generic and can be applied in a number of industries with different quality systems and processes. This is its greatest asset and its greatest liability. Universality itself is its greatest asset, but its application must be tailored to different industries.

Is it difficult to tailor the family of ISO documents for, say, both a hospital and a manufacturing facility? Since the document was written with a manufacturing mindset, a manufacturing application is relatively easy. Applying it to a hospital, though, is more challenging since the language may have to be rewritten to fit those circumstances specific to a hospital setting. Still, the structure, organization, systems, process, objective, and other elements of both types of organizations are similar. For example, both a hospital and manufacturer have customers and want to create quality systems, resources, structure, and processes to increase quality and improve the output of their respective operations.

Assists in Establishing Operational Baselines

All organizations are engaged in a struggle to improve quality. ISO 9000 can be used to baseline, understand, measure, and improve an organization's level of quality performance. ISO 9000 follows an analytical approach of defining and establishing key business processes and systems, such as internal auditing and training. Once established, accepted and approved procedures become operational baselines, ensuring that products conform to specifications.

Operationalizes Quality

Quality is sometimes perceived as the function of a quality group, not of the entire organization. This is a misguided perception. There is no operational ownership. ISO helps to operationalize quality in terms of requiring that procedures and work instructions are developed. Quality has to be operationalized. This requires that work instructions reflect the intent of policies and the requirements of procedures. Quality responsibilities and authorities are defined for all employees. For example, if a problem should occur, an employee can recognize it, initiate actions to fix it, and assure that it doesn't recur. Preferably, the people or team performing a job will be responsible for spelling out what they do and how they do it.

Provides Insights on Organizational Interrelationships

ISO 9000 provides a comprehensive view of an organization's quality systems and the interrelationship among functions. Upon implementing ISO, an organization understands the operational requirements of quality, how they can be applied to a specific process, and how proceduralization can be used to control and manage processes. In many companies, policies and procedures are often written by teams representing different areas. Work instructions are written by people who actually perform the work. The effort of developing the quality manual and the supporting documentation structure reveals how one organizational group's efforts impact others' efforts.

Encourages an Internal Focus

ISO implementation is an exercise in understanding your organization. Developing documentation, specifically work instructions, forces attention to detail. The people performing a job address the quality elements of it and determine the manner in which the work should be performed. Each person has to define, rethink, perhaps even redefine his or her work. Operational processes are defined, documented, and critiqued at each step and at each level. Quality is no longer an abstract idea removed from the realities of daily operations. Rather, it becomes integral to all day-to-day activities.

Does this mean that once operations are documented they can't be changed or modified? No. ISO quality documentation is not written in stone. If circumstances change, then documentation and procedures change to reflect the improvements.

Facilitates Internal Operational Control

ISO quality system requirements emphasize design control, change-order control, and document control. Briefly, design control ensures that the design meets customer's requirements. Change-order control assures that design changes are monitored and approved. Document control ensures the delivery of the right documents to the right people at the right time.

The purpose of internal control is to confirm that operations, systems and process are documented, monitored, stable, and meeting the organization's requirements. If an unusual event occurs, the system may become unstable and result in deficiencies. The deficiencies may involve nonconforming products or inadequate customer service.

Effective internal control ensures that this doesn't occur, unless there is an unusual occurrence, in which case the quality system is capable of catching the deviation, bringing the system back into normal operation, and ensuring that the problem does not recur.

Assists Employees in Understanding and Improving Operations

ISO 9000 requires all employees to understand their organizational quality policies, procedures, and work instructions. All organizations want to improve, become more competitive, or even strive to become "world class." "World class" may mean reducing cycle times, eliminating inventories, improving process capability, reducing setup times on machinery, increasing output, or lowering costs. Regardless of the organizational objective, all employees must know how to do their jobs before any productivity or effectiveness goals can be achieved.

Encourages Self-Assessment

Internal audits are a means of improving internal customer satisfaction, which is key to total quality commitment. To maintain the commitment, it's essential to monitor internal customer satisfaction and to encourage positive attitudes. Standard barometers of employees' satisfaction include turnover, complaints, and absenteeism. Unfortunately, these elements are comparable to inspecting products after the fact. Mistakes already have been made and corrections are expensive. A better way is to measure internal customer satisfaction through an internal quality audit as required by ISO 9001. While the results of the audit may be a bitter pill for management, it's an excellent tool for improving internal customer processes and establishing baselines for improvement.[2]

Maintains Internal Consistency

ISO implementation ensures that operations and the resulting products are consistent. The conventional wisdom holds that quality depends on consistency, uniformity, or reliability. While each of these concepts is slightly different, the essential idea is that quality can be ensured if variation among products and services is at the specification target and is consistent around the target. Only then can products conform to requirements so customers inevitably are satisfied.

Controls Processes and Systems

ISO 9000 implementation results in proceduralizing operations. An organization's systems are documented thoroughly, starting with a quality manual, procedures, and work instructions. Some say the level of documentation and proceduralization stymies innovation and improvement. Policies define the quality direction of the organization. Procedures describe approved methods for obtaining quality and ensuring satisfied internal customers. Work instructions state the most efficient and effective ways of doing a job.

ISO 9000 procedures were initially developed to be a tool for operators to monitor, control, and improve their systems and operations. Once employees grasp their systems and processes through writing or providing input into developing the procedures, they can innovate the processes to add more value. The goal is to have processes that are stable, in control, and capable of meeting requirements. Stable processes improve the quality of employees' work life by allowing the operators to monitor and correct the system only if there are unusual occurrences. Otherwise, they would constantly be fixing problems, adjusting the process, measuring out-of-specification parts, moving deficient parts off the line, and stopping and starting the process. Stable processes improve product quality, improve up time, and ease work for operators.

Establishes Operational Controls

ISO 9001/9002/9003 is characterized by customer-supplier "shall" statements. The supplier shall schedule, shall establish, or shall maintain procedures, systems, or other activities. The net effect of these requirements is to establish a set of operational and organizational controls. These controls can be thought of as "good management practices."

Operational controls include design control, management review, contract review, design verification, and document control procedures. The assumption is that if system documentation controls are in place, operating properly, and monitored frequently, then the output—products and services—will comply with requirements.

Makes Internal Operations More Efficient and Effective

ISO 9000 makes internal operations more efficient and effective, but a company does not have to go through registration to obtain the benefits of ISO 9000. The process of looking at your operations, systems, and processes is rewarding in itself. Many companies operate on autopilot—in other words, how things were done yesterday is how things are done today. Unfortunately, procedures may never have been written, or if they were written, are not being followed today.

Ensures that Product Design Changes Are Controlled

Controlling engineering design modifications or revisions is a major concern for many manufacturers. Changes incorporated into engineering drawings after the initial design or during prototype production are expensive to implement because many downstream production processes and activities may have to be revised. Oftentimes, the problem stems from the fact that upstream or downstream systems don't communicate well. For example, engineers may not fully understand customer needs, or suppliers may not be informed of the product's requirements. Design control forces engineers to understand customer requirements and to design products that satisfy these requirements. If requirements change, changes are logically incorporated into the product. The goal is to eliminate surprises such as deficient designs or unreliable supplier components that may result in product recall.

Creates Awareness of the Need for Training

ISO implementation is often the responsibility of line personnel or of high-performance teams. ISO implementation requires training employees on writing procedures on how they perform jobs. Training is also directed to making self-directed groups into problem solvers.[3]

Obstacles to ISO 9000 Implementation

TQM and ISO 9000 are organizational and cultural change initiatives. They are difficult to implement. Some of the implementation challenges typically encountered include:

- "This too shall pass" attitude.
- No drivers for change.
- Belief that reengineering or eliminating non–value-adding work eliminates jobs.
- No support for quality initiative by management.
- Little training or education for changing business environment.
- Reward systems linked to individuals, not teams.
- Unrealistic vision statement.
- Performance objectives are turned into limited, quantifiable goals.
- Nonstatistical thinking.
- New-program burnout.
- Lack of support, training, or clear goals.
- Inactive senior management.
- Resistance to change.[4]

Encourages Operational Problem Solving

ISO 9000 requires that operations, systems, and processes are understood, detailed, and documented. An attitude must evolve where each employee is responsible for his or her process.

The employee thereby becomes a problem solver, discovering the variables that can affect a system or process, monitoring the process for unusual signs. Continuous small improvements lead to long-term improvements and profitability.

EXPERT'S CORNER
Insights and Tips

I have listened to the unsolicited testimonials of executives from small- to medium-sized firms about how "self-discovery" was the most valuable aspect of their pursuit of ISO 9000. Certification became secondary. They and their key personnel became much more of a harmonious team and understood considerably more about what was really occurring versus what they individually thought was occurring. They got back to the basics of how they wanted the business to be run.
NORM SEIFERT, consultant

ISO 9002 benefited All production and staff groups by formalizing and standardizing practices. We had a few reality checks when management thought procedures made sense until they were used and turned out to be joke on the shop floor. ISO 9002 required shop-floor involvement/ buy-in/ownership. The self-assessments encouraged improvements in procedures, training, change-control processes, and consistency among machines.

Improvement in our quality system, coupled with product quality improvements, reduced the need for many inspection-related activities in our manufacturing processes.

Our quarterly management reviews of the quality system have provided some terrific sharing among our departments. We do a quality system health check around four to five ISO 9002 clauses each quarter. Each Black and White Film department rates its effectiveness and shares any concerns with the rest of the organization.
BETH KRENZER, Manager, Black and
White Film Manufacturing,
Eastman Kodak

(continued)

In addition to generating sales from customers who value goods and services produced by a systematic quality process, ISO registration has helped Data General in other ways.

The effort required for a division to pass an ISO 9000 audit is significant. Teams are established to assess the existing quality system against the ISO standard and provide feedback to enhance overall design, manufacturing, and service processes. Departments not only document their processes, they review the interactions and impact they have with other organizations. This effort has several benefits in addition to strengthening process efficiency and reducing waste. It promotes a team environment.

With management's commitment to quality, the team can accomplish significant goals. For example, Data General–Apex employees accepted the challenge and passed the ISO audit ten weeks later. Management commitment and total Apex involvement were the key ingredients.

Implementation of ISO 9000 involves employee morale, facilitates changes in culture, promotes benchmarking between divisions, standardizes quality system management techniques, and improves cross-functional processes by facilitating more open communications. All of these factors have had a direct impact on strengthening the quality of our products and services. Although significant expenses are incurred in implementing an ISO-compliant quality system and maintaining registration, the return of quality investment materializes in the form of cost reductions, process and productivity improvements, and customer satisfaction.

JOANNE MAYO, Corporate ISO
Coordinator, Data General

Large companies with over 500 people have been the firms leading the registration effort. Small companies, however, can benefit greatly from the registration process because often the process of documenting their work instructions and communicating between departments can help the business realize significant gains in productivity. Oftentimes in a small company, the ideas and management beliefs about business processes are in the mind of an individual, such as the owner.

Documenting procedures allows other people in the organization to learn what the owner believes and to comment on it in order to improve it.

Small businesses will probably realize greater external benefits from registration than larger businesses because the perception of the quality of their products will be comparable to that of a large business in the eyes of the consumer.

ANDREW BERGMAN, Certification
Manager, OTS Quality Registrars

In Chapter 5, we look at how implementing and registering ISO 9000 benefits the customer-supplier relationship.

CHAPTER

5

Customer-Supplier Benefits

BRINGING THE BENEFITS OF ISO TO
THE CUSTOMER-SUPPLIER RELATIONSHIP

More senior managers than ever before view sourcing as a fundamental business process with a bottom-line impact. In order to
deliver a quality product, components, subassemblies, and assemblies must be error-free. This requires an integrated team of engineering, manufacturing, quality, and purchasing personnel with a
much longer perspective than they may have had in the past.[1]

External suppliers are treated similarly to internal suppliers of
products and services. The supplier value-added chain is being
managed more efficiently. The critical question is "How is it
done?" Should a company have multiple suppliers or one supplier
per product line? How are suppliers going to be selected, monitored, and improved?

Multiple suppliers of the same product or service can generate
additional variation, which is the cause of poor quality. The logical
alternative is to have just one or only a few suppliers of a product
or service. In this way, the chances of miscommunication or mis-
understanding are lessened.

Having one supplier is a departure from the traditional method
of having multiple suppliers of the same product. Until recently, it
was thought that multiple suppliers could keep prices low and
would serve as a buffer if one or more suppliers could not ship

product. Now it is becoming more common to have one or two suppliers provide a family of products and/or services. This demands that suppliers be integrated with the customer.

Hutchins's Rules of Global Business[2]

There are many critical elements of global business, but the following are some of the most important:

- Please your stakeholders.
- Do what you do best.
- Outsource all other work to "world class" suppliers.
- Acquire processes and systems as well as products.
- Judge "world class" suppliers by quality, cost, and service.
- Innovate and improve continuously.

GROWTH IN CUSTOMER-SUPPLIER PARTNERING

An important element of restructuring is the growth in customer-supplier partnering. Excess paperwork, late deliveries, misunderstandings, poor service, and defective products are no longer acceptable.

The process starts with *everyone*—including external suppliers—understanding the needs of the final customer. Everyone adding value needs to know how their jobs affect or enhance the total satisfaction of the external customer.

At Allison Transmission's manufacturing plant, material receiving is an extension of the company's supplier management organization. The shipping function is an extension of the assembly organization and thereby eliminates production and material control groups. More of Allison's processes start as independent operations and evolve to become extensions of one another until there is seamless integration. To facilitate this process, Allison has trained production generalists instead of specialists. The factory will eventually be linked with its suppliers so that design information and production scheduling will be electronically transmitted.[3]

Do customers initiate this process with just any supplier? Often customers want to work with progressive, "world class" suppliers. "World class" means the supplier has survived a prolonged evaluation and certification process. Most major companies, have supplier certification initiatives that analyze reams of information obtained from supplier assessments, product evaluations, technical/engineering testing, and other assessments. Depending on the result of these evaluations, a supplier is placed on the continuous-improvement treadmill, which is necessary if that supplier is to be on the approved bid list for new work.[4]

ISO 9000 facilitates customer-supplier partnering through the following:

- Forms the basis for a common language of quality.
- Ensures a minimum level of quality.
- Facilitates development of seamless operations.
- Reduces the supplier base.
- Facilitates just-in-time delivery.
- Assists in selecting suppliers.
- Assists in monitoring suppliers.
- Assists in training suppliers.

Forms the Basis for a Common Language of Quality

An important TQM principle is the concept of the customer and supplier working together to add value. The process begins within the organization and then extends outward into the supplier base.

The goal is to develop mutually beneficial relationships among all parties in order to please the final customer with high-quality, cost-competitive products and services. ISO 9001/9002/9003 provides the foundation of a common language and the structure for developing a Total Quality Management program.

Ensures a Minimum Level of Quality

More business is being pushed onto the supplier base as companies focus on their core competencies, on what they do well. A company may have thousands of domestic and offshore suppliers, and the question is how does a customer ensure that all its suppliers have a minimum level of quality. ISO 9000 audits throughout the world are similar and soon will be recognized worldwide. Comparable audits should indicate that registered suppliers are maintaining at least a minimum level of quality.

Facilitates Development of Seamless Operations

Functional departments such as Engineering and Manufacturing have been the traditional base for managing, organizing, planning, and reporting on work. The problem is that organizational hierarchies and specializations grew that sometimes hindered the development of new ideas or hindered the flow of work. Companies are now organizing work by natural systems and processes, such as those addressed in ISO 9000. The goal is to have a seamless transfer of resources. ISO 9000 assists in structuring operations so critical quality systems are established, controls are set in place, procedures are written, and systems are monitored. If unusual deviations or variations occur, then controls correct the deviation.

Reduces the Supplier Base

Quality, cost, technology, and delivery criteria are the means to determine with whom partnerships will be developed. ISO 9000 operational criteria are often used as the first-level criteria. The process of partnering follows a pattern with suppliers first becoming accepted, approved, and then certified. The goal at each step of the certification process is to evaluate the prospective partner. At each step, the supplier is induced towards partnership with more work. At the highest certification level, the supplier is fully integrated with the customer.

During the certification process, the supplier base shrinks. The remaining suppliers partner with the customer. In this economy, customers can be very selective about the businesses with whom they want to partner. The long-term goal is a mutually rewarding relationship with one or two suppliers per commodity or product line.

Facilitates Just-in-Time Delivery

A Boeing 747, the world's largest commercial airliner, rolls off the production line every four days. The 747 has 6 million separate components, sourced from 1,500 different suppliers in 15 countries. Scheduling, quality, quantity, cost, and reliability are extremely critical. In terms of sequenced delivery, there is no room to store excess wings and fuselages; parts are delivered just as they are used.[5]

ISO 9000–registered suppliers have systems in place to establish that high quality is maintained. If problems occur, they are resolved quickly. This facilitates the smooth flow of material to customers, in the proper sequence to be used, and just-in-time to be used. This is especially important to customers who have many sourced materials and products.

Assists in Selecting Suppliers

As customer requirements increase, companies are relying on "world class" suppliers to produce products or deliver services. Suppliers are required to have extensive quality systems in place before a full partnership can develop. Partnering can serve as the basis for future trust and further cooperation.

ISO quality requirements are being pushed further downstream into the supplier base in many industries. For example, the U.S. auto industry is harmonizing its diverse customer-supplier certifications to ISO 9000. ISO 9000 registration will become critical if not mandatory if suppliers want to be on many approved bidder's lists.

Assists in Monitoring Suppliers

Quality initiatives within vertical industry sectors have much in common. For example, the automotive, chemical, medical supply, and pressure vessel industries share common quality standards, specifications, manuals, and certification documents. Customers audit the same industry suppliers the same way. This creates redundancy and adds costs to both the customer and supplier. The customer must send personnel to conduct the audits. The supplier must assign personnel to assist the customer audit team, and also runs the risk of having operations disrupted.

The following approach makes more sense. Say there is a U.S. customer who knows of a supplier in Sri Lanka that provides unique products or services, and the customer wants to know whether this supplier has the minimum quality systems. If the U.S. customer could check a registry of companies in Sri Lanka to determine whether the supplier has been registered, the customer could avoid having to conduct his own audit, but still receive at least some level of assurance that the supplier has quality systems.

Assists in Training Suppliers

Companies are integrating suppliers into key operations. Preferred supplier-partners produce defect-free products, shrink delivery lead times, improve product designs, and lower costs. John Deere evaluates suppliers in terms of quality-assurance programs, pricing, just-in-time delivery, engineering support, handling of warranty problems, and sales expertise. Suppliers scoring high are rewarded with more work. This type of development requires that companies invest in training.[6]

Often, customers provide key suppliers with ISO 9000, internal auditing, statistical process control (SPC), and other types of training. The objective of this training is to bring the customer and suppliers closer together. The customer understands its supplier capabilities and how they can be improved. The supplier understands its customer's needs.

EXPERT'S CORNER
Insights and Tips

Black and White Film Manufacturing relied on numerous internal [Kodak] suppliers for materials and services. Internal suppliers provided everything from the clear plastic base that black-and-white film is coated with to maintenance service. We also found our ISO 9002 journey forced us to unify our approach for specifying supplier requirements for quality/ cost/ of products and services they provided. We found that historically we did not communicate as consistently or formally with our own internal suppliers as we had with external suppliers. To correct this, we wrote interface agreements with internal suppliers.

Many suppliers (especially our fellow Kodakers) kicked and screamed about the added perceived bureaucracy. Many suppliers felt we were asking for the moon and, after all, these suppliers were not intending to go for ISO 9002 themselves.

What started as a perceived lay-on ended up benefiting our suppliers. Suppliers had a clearer idea of Black and White Film Manufacturing's expectations. Suppliers were also assessed by our trained ISO internal auditors. Assessments by Black and White Film provided valuable improvement opportunities to suppliers. In addition, the corrective action process Black and White undertook for ISO 9002 provided a great way to track supplier-caused problems in services/products and to close the loop on supplier corrective action. ISO 9002 registration also provided the platform and impetus for positive customer-supplier communication and improved relations.

BETH KRENZER, Manager, Black and
White Film Manufacturing,
Eastman Kodak

CHAPTER

6

Getting Started

Every moment spent planning saves three or four in execution.
CRAWFORD GREENWALT, President,
Du Pont

ISO 9000 registration is a basic quality initiative comprising open communication, extensive training, solid documentation, and other commonsense management principles. The process of registration or implementation is not difficult, but common sense must be applied.

ISO 9000 incorporates critical elements of several quality approaches. As a family of quality systems, ISO 9000 is similar to the Malcolm Baldrige National Quality Award and comparable international awards. While ISO 9000 doesn't include the highest-quality practices, it does represent the most common ones. It requires that quality policies, procedures, and work instructions are written and adhered to.

JUST DO IT

Should you just implement ISO 9000 or go through the process of becoming registered? The decision eventually will be based on a number of factors, as described below.

The process of securing ISO 9000 registration can be broken down into the following stages: (1) preregistration, (2) registration,

What's the Best Way to Start?

Is there one best way for implementing a quality initiative? No. Probably the best approach is to integrate elements of several approaches. A recent study identified seven strategies or approaches for implementing a total continuous quality-improvement initiative:

- *Quality award criteria,* such as the Malcolm Baldrige National Quality Award, the European Quality Award, etc.

- *"World class"* or best in benchmarking practices.

- *Employee empowerment,* involvement, or self-directed team approach.

- *Customer-supplier-driven improvement,* such as ISO 9000, Ford's Q 101, or Motorola's Six Sigma.

- *Total Quality Management systems approach,* involving ISO 9000 elements.

- *Japanese total-quality approach,* involving Kaizen, QFD, and other Japanese tools.

- *Guru approach,* involving Juran, Feigenbaum, Crosby, or Deming.[1]

and (3) postregistration. While a company may not want to become registered, much value can be gained from just setting up a quality and operational structure based on ISO 9000 quality systems. If you are only interested in becoming registered, then follow all the steps outlined below. If you are only interested in implementing ISO 9000 internally, then follow the steps in the first stage, preregistration. Regardless of whether or not you're pursuing registration, just implementing the process provides many internal, marketing, and customer-supplier benefits.

PREREGISTRATION

Preregistration entails understanding ISO 9000 requirements and assessing what needs to be done to close the gap between "where one is" and "where one should be" in order to comply with ISO 9001/9002/9003.

The following steps may be followed if an organization wants to adopt the ISO standard and obtain the benefits from proceduralizing operations:

1. Understand globalization of business.

2. Understand ISO 9000 standards and guidelines.

3. Talk to customers.

4. Benchmark competition.

5. Identify internal baselines.

6. Talk with stakeholders.

7. Obtain top-management support.

8. Attend a registration seminar.

9. Establish a team.

10. Develop a project scope, schedule, plan, and estimate.

11. Retain an ISO consultant.

12. Conduct a preassessment.

13. Upgrade quality documentation and other quality system elements.

14. Overcome obstacles and resistance.

15. Evaluate and improve internal quality controls.

Understand Globalization of Business

The nature of trade is dramatically changing as the economic world becomes increasing divided into free-trade market areas and managed trading blocs. What does this mean for the average small and medium-sized business? The ways in which products are going to be sold will change. International and domestic customers will want objective and independent assurance that they are getting what they paid for. Product testing, ISO registration, or other methods to determine conformity to customer requirements may be required. Customers want to minimize the risks of obtaining nonconforming products, so they will require some type of independent, third-party assessment such as product testing or quality systems registration. These requirements may help or hinder you from selling your products.

Understand ISO 9000 Standards and Guidelines

There is no alternative to fully understanding the entire array of ISO 9000 documents. It's most important to understand the "shall" ISO 9001/9002/9003 documents, but an organization should also purchase and understand the remaining "should" documents, as these guidelines show how ISO 9001/9002/9003 can be applied effectively.

Talk to Customers

What do or will customers require in terms of your providing product or quality systems assurance? It is not as simple as getting this information from your immediate customer, which may be either the end user or a commercial buyer. You may have to go further upstream to your customer's customer to determine future requirements.

ISO 9000 requirements are spreading quickly in different industry sectors. A customer may require ISO registration not just of its immediate supplier, but also of the *supplier's* supplier, and so on down the supplier chain. This is not only on a national level; regional authorities, such as the European Community or other trading blocs, may also establish requirements.

Benchmark Competition

What is your competition doing? One way to obtain information about ISO registration is to inquire about various business operations, systems, and processes in your own as well as other industry sectors. Information can be obtained through clearinghouses, published sources, surveys, consultants, one-on-one discussions, trade/professional group collaboration, electronic databases, and industry observers.

Find out how AT&T, Du Pont, Eastman Kodak, and others have implemented ISO 9000 and how they use it to remain competitive. Comparisons can be conducted against internal operations, against best-in-class within an industry, or against operations outside an industry.

How do you find what larger companies did to attain registration? If you're a supplier or customer, you may be able to attend one of their in-house ISO classes. Otherwise, check out some of the many large organizations that allow other companies to attend their ISO seminars.

Identify Internal Baselines

Internal baselines identify your organization's current status in terms of quality systems, processes, or products. This process identifies the "what is" status of your organization's quality systems, which is then compared against best-in-class firms on a worldwide basis. The difference between the best and an organization's baselines serves as the gap that must be closed. Metrics, or measurements, are essential in pursuing implementation or registration.

Talk with Stakeholders

Stakeholders are ISO-interested parties, such as customers, auditors, government authorities, trade groups, ISO consultants, registrars, and accreditors. By talking with these groups, you obtain the following benefits:

- Understanding of the full range of options available to you.

- Knowledge of the perspectives of the different stakeholders.

- Observation of the knowledge and skill levels of the different groups.

Obtain Top-Management Support

Top management must buy in and actively support the registration process. One of the requirements of the "management responsibility" quality system is that the supplier must appoint a management representative responsible for ensuring compliance with the standard. Top management needs to keep abreast of what is going on with their company's ISO implementation, as it can radically change the way a business operates.

Top management should also be intimately involved because ISO implementation or registration requires:

- Allocating resources.

- Establishing guidelines and direction for the organization.

- Evaluating current operations.

- Developing and writing procedures and instructions.

- Implementing changes and measuring improvements.

Attend a Registration Seminar.

Hundreds of registration seminars are offered each year. These seminars cover the "what is" and "how to" involved in becoming registered. They are a good investment because they reveal how to become registered simply and quickly. Why not learn from others' processes and mistakes?

Another option is to send key people to a five-day training class conducted by a lead auditor. This class is required of all quality system auditors who will conduct ISO audits, and illustrates what the registrar looks for and how the registrar's auditors conduct the audit.

Communicating the Importance of ISO

Good communications is especially important in quality management. In too many cases, quality promises are made and not delivered. Communications strategy should be carefully planned and coordinated to support ISO 9000 implementation or registration.

A strategy may require that you:

- Identify the objectives, plans, and strategies of the ISO registration and/or implementation.

- Examine and understand the key issues to emerge from the registration and/or implementation of ISO.

- Analyze the key messages to explain and support the quality effort.

- Determine who the audience of the message is.

- Identify the best media through which to deliver the messages.

- Monitor and support the communications effort.

- Encourage stakeholder feedback to support, reinforce, and, if required, change the quality message.[2]

Establish a Team

ISO implementation or registration can be thought of in terms of developing a product. A multidisciplinary team is formed with strict responsibilities and tight time lines. Who should be on it? The team can comprise people from Product Design, Manufacturing, and Servicing. As a general rule, it should include everyone who can contribute to an efficient process.

Develop a Project Scope, Schedule, Plan, and Estimate

The project team should develop a project scope, schedule, plan of action, and costs estimate. The scope reveals which plants or operations will be registered. The schedule allows the organization to allocate resources for registration. The plan of action describes who does, what, where, and when. The estimate identifies the internal and external costs of registration. With these elements in place, management and the organization can estimate the costs and identify the benefits of registration.

Retain an ISO consultant

A reputable consultant can lead you through the registration process, advise you how to navigate the course effectively and economically, without chasing false leads, and provide you with information about many other value-added activities. He or she will also be able to conduct or help you conduct a preassessment.

Conduct a Preassessment

The preassessment compares "what is" against "what should be" as specified in the particular ISO document. This analysis sometimes is called a preliminary audit or a gap analysis. The gap is the amount of work necessary to achieve the level of quality that would allow the organization to pass an audit the first time through. The important point is that you should be involved regardless of whomever conducts the audit. It is your quality system and processes.

At a simple level, registration requires determining what the ISO quality system requirements are; evaluating what one is doing in regard to these quality systems; determining variances between the "shall" and the "should," and closing the gap between the two.

The preassessment will identify shortcomings in the quality system, including documentation, training, methods, equipment, or other factors. It can be conducted by the auditee, auditor (registrar), or consultant.

In general, the preassessment should:

- Verify audit readiness.

- Identify the resources necessary to pass the audit.

- Instill confidence about passing the audit.

Upgrade Quality Documentation and Other Quality System Elements

The major ISO shortcoming for many organizations is lack of documentation. While organizations may have a decorative quality manual, too often quality systems have not been incorporated and integrated throughout the organization. ISO implementation requires that all critical quality activities be understood, documented, and controlled.

A fundamental element of control is establishing consistent operations so uniform products are produced. Consistency is verified by developing procedures and documentation for all critical tasks involving quality.

Overcome Obstacles and Resistance

Cynicism, turf battles, lack of time, and lack of knowledge are just some of the obstacles to ISO implementation or registration. Others exist as well. Sometimes, for example, top management is not visibly or actively supportive of registration. One individual or a small team may be responsible for registration and may not have the political capital or resources to carry it off. Or the union or some other important stakeholder may not have been brought on board. All of these can crush or stifle the registration effort.

Evaluate and Improve Internal Quality Controls

Internal controls confirm that operations are consistent so deficiencies don't occur. If they do occur, then internal controls such as corrective-action feedback loops ensure that they don't recur.

REGISTRATION

Registration does not have to be pursued for a company to obtain the benefits of ISO implementation. The major advantage of registration is that an independent and objective third-party evaluates and "blesses" your systems and places your company on a register everyone can see. The list of accrued benefits are listed in Chapter 4.

The steps in the registration stage are:

1. Talk to registrars.

2. Select a registrar.

3. Complete the registration application and questionnaire.

4. Negotiate terms and understand conditions.

5. Plan the audit jointly.

6. Schedule the audit.

7. Cooperate and coordinate with the auditor.

Talk to Registrars

There are more than 30 accredited ISO registrars in the United States. Which is the best for you? The answer involves analyzing many factors, including:

- Registrar's background and specialty.
- Experience and knowledge of the registrar's personnel.
- Registrar's scope of activities.
- Registrar's testing facilities.
- Length of time before an audit can be conducted.
- Chemistry and trust between registrar and company.

Overcoming Resistance

ISO registration and implementation involves change and requires action. The following ten reasons are often heard for not pursuing action, including not pursuing registration:

- It's never been done or tried before.
- In won't work here (i.e., small company, big company, schools, R/D, etc.).
- This is just the latest flavor of the month.
- Why fix it if it ain't broke.
- Our customers aren't asking for it and our competitors aren't doing it.
- It costs too much and causes too much trouble.
- We're different than our competition.
- It can't, shouldn't, and won't be done.
- It's not my job, problem, etc.
- Let's develop consensus (i.e., from management, union, etc.).

Your relationship with the registrar likely will be a long-term one. The registrar will be surveillance-auditing you every six months and will conduct a complete reaudit every three years. The relationship should be based on trust, courtesy, and confidentiality.

Select a registrar

The registrar is selling a service. The service itself, as well as trust, courtesy, delivery, and total cost, should be considered in the decision. Low cost alone should not dictate the choice of a registrar. Total cost should be one of several requirements to be factored into the selection decision.

Complete the Registration Application and Questionnaire

The registration application is a formal document providing the registrar with information about the applicant. It includes background information, fee structure, client list, and a request for quality documentation.

The registrar uses the application to obtain information about your processes. If you have specialized products or processes, the registrar must evaluate his or her ability to audit your facility, as those specialized processes may require the registrar to obtain specific training or to retain a specialist to accompany the audit team. The registrar will also ask for a quality manual, specifications, procedures, or work instructions, to help develop a questionnaire for planning and conducting the audit.

Negotiate Terms and Understand Conditions

Many elements surrounding ISO 9000 are negotiable, including scope of services and consultation, costs, and use of the registrar's symbols. Let's discuss these. The registrar offers a number of services, some of which are consulting, auditing, and training. The registrar under a separate division may also provide training of the best methods for achieving registration. Registration costs are fairly standard and often are based on a per diem charge. Finally, the registrar owns a logo, trademark, and other symbols. These symbols convey trust and credibility of the registrar's authority, so the registrar prescribes how the registrant uses them.

Plan the Audit Jointly

The registration audit should be planned jointly by the registrar and you. The wait for an audit may be up to six months long. During this period, plan and prepare for the audit. The registrar should inform you what will be evaluated and who should be available for interviews.

Schedule the Audit

The registrar's audit team will visit your facilities, observe tests, interview personnel, analyze information, and evaluate quality systems, during which time the team may unintentionally disrupt operations. It's important that these requirements are identified before the audit.

Cooperate and Coordinate with the Auditor

The audit team evaluates your quality systems in order to gather evidence to determine compliance with the applicable ISO 9001/9002/9003 quality system requirements. The auditor may:

- *Check your quality manual.* This determines whether all the quality elements of the particular ISO standard are addressed.

- *Evaluate procedures.* This ascertains whether procedures have been written for each of the quality systems.

- *Interview people.* This determines whether top management is actively involved in the quality initiative; whether a management representative has been selected to lead the effort; whether procedures have been written to reflect how things are done as opposed to how they should be done; whether employees understand what they are doing; whether work instructions are being followed and personnel has been trained properly.

- *Observe operations.* This verifies that operations are running according to written procedures.

- *Verify systems.* This ensures that a quality system, such as corrective action, is fixing the problem as well as eliminating the root cause of the deficiency.

- *Analyze documents.* This determines whether all the elements of the applicable ISO systems requirement have been met.

POSTREGISTRATION

The goal of the postregistration stage is to ensure that subsequent relations between the registrar and registrant are smooth and courteous. Registration is just the first step in a long-term registrar-registrant relationship. Every six months or once a year, the registrar conducts a surveillance audit of your facilities, and every three years, a full reaudit.

The steps in the postregistration stage are:

1. Schedule a meeting with the auditor.
2. Correct deficiencies.
3. Pursue continuous improvement.
4. Maintain registration.
5. Anticipate surveillance visits.
6. Apply for registration.

Schedule a Meeting with the Auditor

Meetings should be scheduled with the auditor at critical junctures. Upon completion of the audit, request an immediate meeting while the auditor and team are still on the premises.

The purpose of the postaudit meeting is to discuss preliminary findings and corrective actions. If a large facility is being audited, meetings may be scheduled at the end of day. The meetings facilitate communication and deter misunderstandings, surprises, or differences. For example, the auditor may have misinterpreted some drawings or not interviewed the proper personnel.

Correct Deficiencies

The auditor will issue corrective action requests (CAR) for deficiencies the audit team has discovered. The deficiencies, or sometimes called nonconformances, indicate that quality systems or other elements do not comply with the applicable ISO 9001/9002/9003 system requirements. You are responsible for correcting any deficiencies.

Pursue Continuous Improvement

The maintenance of the registration requires paying daily attention to your systems, processes, and products. If they are not monitored and controlled, variation increases.

ISO registration is not static. The registrar reaudits your quality systems every six months. The auditors will verify that problems don't recur. Corrective action will fix the symptom and the cause so the problem does not persist in the same or some other form. The long-term goal is to confirm that your operations and quality systems undergo continuous improvement.

Maintain Registration

Registration is maintained as long as conditions between the registrar and you are satisfied, specifically:

- Quality documentation is controlled in compliance with ISO requirements.

- You notify the registrar if there are major system changes.

- You provide access so auditors can conduct the audit.

- One of your executives is responsible for certification activities.

- Registrar's trademarks are used only in specified ways.

Anticipate Surveillance Visits

Every six months or once a year, the registrar will audit part of your quality systems. These audits are announced and planned according to the registration certificate and contract. The registrar wants to work with you. He or she doesn't want a reputation for being easy, nonprofessional, or too difficult. The registrar wants to encourage business but not lose his or her own accreditation. It's a fine line.

A registrar can suspend registration under the following circumstances:

- Fraud or negligence is discovered.

- Corrective actions are not being followed.

- Trademarks or other symbols are being misused.

Apply for Recertification

Every three years or so, you may have to be fully recertified. All of the company's quality systems will be reaudited to the latest ISO standards. This is a voluntary requirement among registrars. Some registrars don't require this of registered companies.

THE EXPERT'S CORNER
Insights and Tips

Suckle Corporation took a classic Juran approach to ISO implementation and treated the ISO quality system implementation as an improvement project. The staff (heads of Operations, Engineering, Accounting, Marketing and Sales, and Quality), led by the president and vice president of the company, formed a steering committee for process improvement. Each group then took an active role in the improvement project they sponsored. The following were the critical passages in our ISO journey.

TRAINING

We began the process by training the vice president and the quality manager as ISO lead assessors and appointing them as ISO representative and coordinator, respectively. Next, four internal auditors were trained to assist in the systems analysis phase. As implementation progressed, we trained an additional four lead assessors from the Quality, Engineering, Customer Service, and Manufacturing areas to assure both understanding and commitment on the part of all functional areas.

Finally, in the implementation phase of the project, all users were trained in the use of quality manuals, procedures, or other subsystems by walking through the new system under the tutelage of a lead assessor.

SYSTEMS ANALYSIS

The current quality system (a derivative of ISO 9002) was compared to the standard to determine the extent of the work needed to comply with the standard and to schedule implementation. A detailed procedure describing the system analysis methodologies to be used was issued to key personnel across all departments as a training aid for the next phase of the project.

At the earliest stage of implementation, a project management plan was drawn up and issued to the participants. Each team was responsible for updating the plan weekly. Project Evaluation and Review Technique (PERT) was key in bringing the implementation in on time using the very limited resources available.

(continued)

USER INTERVIEWS

The first element of the process improvement/systems analysis approach was the involvement of the users of the system. The implementation team was tasked with drafting a procedure that met the intent of the standard and taking it to the people who would use it. In these initial interviews, the ISO team flowcharted both the current process and the new procedure. Brainstorming with the users would then take place to determine the impact of the ISO procedure on the way the users operated. In these first encounters, most of the real work of systems analysis got done.

USER-FRIENDLY PROCEDURES

Because of the process used to develop procedures, they came out of the gate as "user friendly." This created a much more open and rapid deployment of the procedures into the business system.

WALKTHROUGH

Even though the procedures were "user friendly," a walkthrough of each procedure was performed before final deployment. The walkthrough consisted of lead assessors and those with functional responsibility for developing and monitoring the use of the procedure. If required, employees were coached or the procedures were modified prior to final approval of the procedure. This method ensured that the procedure not only met the intent of the standard, but could be applied to the system with no negative effect on the other elements of the system. The walkthrough served as the basis for system-wide ISO training and implementation.

IMPLEMENTATION

After each walkthrough, the results were analyzed by the team and the procedures were either marked for implementation or the correction cycle was applied. In either case, the project-by-project, task-by-task tracking method was used and the entire process reported to the steering committee. As each element became a part of the quality system, it underwent weekly qualification audits for the first 30 days of use and stayed at that frequency until three audits with no discrepancies were performed. After qualification, the procedure reverted to the normal frequency for auditing as specified in the quality manual.

> JOHN ZAVACKI, QA Manager,
> Suckle Corporation

Establish communication networks within the company or with other companies on approaches and issues. Though many areas within Kodak Park are obtaining separate registration, we have established an extensive communication network relying on a monthly meeting and intra-company electronic mail. The initial role of this group was to better understand the requirements of the standard, especially as it relates to photographic manufacturing areas. We then developed a common understanding of the key steps in implementing a quality system. As areas started detailed implementation, we addressed specific issues and established a common understanding of the path ahead. With many of our material and service suppliers internal to the company but outside the scope of the individual registrations, there were many questions regarding how we could best ensure the quality of these materials and services. We established common approaches and formats that have been used throughout the organization. As areas have achieved registration, we have continued to share the observations of the third-party auditors. As a result we have been told several times by these auditors that if they find a nonconformance in one organization, it is very rare they will find it in another area on a subsequent audit.

We also learned the following from our implementation:

- *ISO is not a contest to see who can generate the most paperwork. Actually, the winners are those who can effectively comply to the standard with less!*

- *Try to build on what others have done, but make the quality system work for you. Someone else's quality system may look great, but not fit your organization's needs.*

(continued)

- *This is not a task for a SWAT team from another area. Leadership must come from the top and everyone must be involved.*

- *Keep in mind why you're doing the work. The purpose is improved quality of your products and services.*

- *Monument builders—stay away! Good quality systems require minimum maintenance, they don't provide jobs for a staff of document coordinators and records keepers.*

- *If you're going to fret over the cost, don't start. Obtaining and retaining ISO registration requires the investment of a significant amount of time for training, implementation, and verification.*

- *Before selecting a third-party auditor, talk with others who have worked with them. Identify their strengths and weaknesses as they relate to your needs.*

- *Establish a time line and stick to it. Delaying the date set for the initial audit only results in more delay in getting the necessary work done.*

KAREN LOVECCHIO,
ISO 9000 Coordinator,
Kodak Park Division,
Eastman Kodak

Eastman Kodak's Black and White Film Manufacturing division successfully pursued ISO 9002 registration and implementation. We learned the following from its experience.

LESSONS LEARNED

- *It's your quality system and you will have to live with the good, bad, and ugly after you get registered.*

- *People doing the work need to own the quality system.*

- *Professionals and other "day workers" can be the most difficult to get to document their practices and be "controlled."*

- *Reinforce the behaviors you want in your quality system—the results will come!*

IT'S IMPORTANT TO . . .

- *Have a grass-roots team working at least part time on ISO.*

- *Get management involvement (a steering team).*

- *Know when to cut bait—don't go wild on elaborate systems.*

- *Analyze areas in which you think ISO 9000 will improve your quality and productivity, and track progress to show ISO has* internal *benefits.*

- *Log customer inquiries about your ISO 9000 status/program. This can be important to drive sales and your quality reputation.*

- *Know what your competitors are doing relative to ISO 9000.*

PURSUE THE WIN/WIN

- *Figure out how to marry ISO 9000 with your other initiatives. For example, the Black and White division has had many inquiries from our customers in the health-care field (regarding our ISO status for medical films) and from customers in the printing and publishing businesses (regarding ISO registration for films and printing plates). We provided copies of our registration certificates and quality manuals to customers. We have coached customers on quality systems like ISO 9000, problem-solving tools, TQM, and team building. Our goal is to empower Kodak customers with the tools and knowledge through which they can improve their quality, service, and productivity . . . a WIN/WIN.*

BETH KRENZER, Manager,
Black and White Film
Manufacturing, Eastman Kodak

(continued)

Data General was the first major U.S. computer manufacturer to have all its worldwide manufacturing operations ISO 9002 certified and is among the first major U.S. suppliers of open system platforms to have its full design, manufacture, service, and support cycle ISO registered.

Data General's success story of becoming certified to ISO 9000 Quality System Standards is one that other companies could benefit from before attempting registration. Its success is attributed to a phased approach. First, individual divisions within the company attained registration independently, instead of a company-wide attempt. Second, Data General has begun to use the process definitions from the ISO programs to reengineer the way the company operates. Their focused approach resulted in a successful quality program.

JOANNE MAYO, Corporate ISO
Coordinator, Data General

Small companies, especially those with fewer than 50 employees, sometimes don't have a QA department. While ISO 9000 does not require the establishment of a QA department, an individual does have to be responsible for assuring that requirements of the standard are met. If they do form a QA department, the interrelationship of this department with other personnel and departments must be defined. Often when a small company grows and forms a QA department, the roles and responsibilities of the QA department are often not defined in such areas as design review and inspection and test records. In most cases, these activities were previously controlled entirely by the project manager.

ANDREW BERGMAN, Certification
Manager, OTS Quality Registrars,

PART II

Discussion of Specific ISO 9001 Quality System Requirements

The second part of *Taking Care of Business* examines the 20 quality system requirements of ISO 9001. Each of the 20 requirements is covered in basically the same format. The critical quality requirement, or clause, is first explained in the section entitled "Quick Scan—ISO 9001 Requirements," after which its importance, value, and purpose is discussed. Next comes examples of how the requirement can be used to make your organization more efficient and effective. Each section closes with probably the most important benefit of this book, the honest and revealing tips of people who have worked with the quality system requirement under discussion. In the "Expert's Corner" section, consultants, registrars, and implementers share their tips and suggestions on implementing each quality system requirement.

Part II covers the following quality system requirements:

4.1 Management Responsibility

4.2 Quality Systems

4.3   Contract Review

4.4   Design Control

4.5   Document Control

4.6   Purchasing

4.7   Purchaser-Supplied Product

4.8   Product Identification and Traceability

4.9   Process Control

4.10   Inspection and Testing

4.11   Inspection, Measuring, and Test Equipment

4.12   Inspection and Test Status

4.13   Control of Nonconforming Product

4.14   Corrective Action

4.15   Handling, Storage, Packaging, and Delivery

4.16   Quality Records

4.17   Internal Quality Audits

4.18   Training

4.19   Servicing

4.20   Statistical Techniques

4.1

Management Responsibility

The [quality control] issue has more to do with people and motivation and less to do with capital and equipment than one would think. It involves a cultural change.

MICHAEL BEER, professor

QUICK SCAN
ISO 9001 Requirements

Quality policies and objectives are defined, understandable, and doable. Management shows its commitment to the pursuit of the organization's quality objectives by monitoring compliance of the quality policy, actively reinforcing quality policies, and not accepting deviations from written policies.

Each employee knows his or her job. Quality authorities and responsibilities are spelled out and understood. A designated company representative monitors and reports on the level of quality. This person assesses standards, training, equipment, procedures, and schedules.

Management periodically reviews the quality system, including staffing, policies, procedures, objectives, customer feedback, internal audits, process performance, and product performance. The frequency of the review is also evaluated. Chronic problems, including high-risk and systemic problem areas, are assessed more frequently.

IMPORTANCE OF MANAGEMENT RESPONSIBILITY

Management responsibility is the foundation and the driver of all
the other quality system requirements. Management responsibility
specifically covers the following areas:

- *Quality policy* ensures that quality objectives and plans and
  other statements communicate the organization's commitment to quality and to customer satisfaction.

- *Responsibility and authority* affirm that policies are implemented
  so everyone in the organization can achieve quality objectives
  and fulfill quality requirements.

- *Verification resources and personnel* are organizational elements
  to assure that quality is properly documented and supported.
  These elements may include trained personnel, accurate
  specifications, proper training, documented procedures, and
  calibrated equipment.

- *Management representative* is a person who is ultimately responsible for ensuring contractual requirements are satisfied.

- *Management review* is a periodic structured assessment of quality systems to confirm that requirements are being satisfied.
  Reviews may assess the structure of the quality system, end-
  product quality, staffing requirements, and internal feedback
  mechanisms.

TOP-MANAGEMENT SUPPORT

Top management is the architect of an organization's quality
system. ISO 9000 will work only if top management is directly
involved and committed to the development, implementation,
and registration of its quality systems.

The organization's quality policy is the cornerstone of the quality system. In a quality policy, the organization states its vision, values, and beliefs for its major stakeholders, including employees, customers, suppliers, community, regulatory bodies, and others. The organization's vision and mission statements must reflect the realities of the organization. If they don't, organizational dysfunction occurs. In other words, the reality of what is said and done contradict each other. As a result, employees become cynical and resist the ISO systems and processes of change, which may be proceduralizing operations or following up on corrective action.

Policy is then translated to workable procedures, which are the second level of the documentation hierarchy. Procedures are the action guidelines of the organization's quality system. Procedures are developed by people who have the knowledge and experience to state and write what actually occurs in their organization.

Strategies and plans are drafted to support the quality effort and are expressed in terms the organization can understand. Quality service standards and procedures, as well as desired levels of performance, are thoroughly described. Statements such as "error-free or zero-defect performance" cannot simply be tossed to people as performance standards. Performance requirements must describe and detail "what is" expected and "how to" achieve them.

Top-management support is necessary if ISO or any quality initiative is to succeed. ISO 9001 specifically requires that a management representative be appointed to oversee compliance. Senior management must regard quality as a top priority of the organization's competitiveness and survivability.

QUALITY CULTURE

Organizational culture, the basic belief system of an organization, has to be conducive to and reinforce the quality ethic. Otherwise, the quality initiative will self-destruct, and ISO implementation becomes a waste of time and money.

The quality ethic has penetrated and been adopted by many big companies. However, with many small American companies, the process has been slow. Often, these companies can't afford training in quality because their main concern is simply survival. It is difficult to go beyond the superficial words of "We believe in quality." Clear values and beliefs must foster quality behavior.

What can be done to ensure that the quality culture and leadership are aligned? Management can:

- Communicate the quality vision and mission to employees.

- Empower employees through interdisciplinary, process improvement, self-directed, and corrective action teams.

- Assess, monitor, and internalize the voice of the customer.

- Partner with companies where there are natural synergies and advantages.[1]

QUALITY POLICY

An organization defines its quality culture and commitment through its quality policies. The typical quality policy may state that an organization "anticipates and exceeds customers' requirements and expectations through cost-competitive products and services that are delivered on time every time."

Quality policies, commitment, and actions are aligned with one another. Quality policy reflects the organization's culture, people, and products. A written quality policy identifies the objectives of the quality initiative and the individuals responsible for decision making regarding quality. The mandate for quality is derived from the customer and is articulated by the chief executive officer.

If there is no quality commitment, it is much more difficult to implement an organizational change. The total-quality ethic can mean a radical departure from business as usual to a systematic integration of quality and customer throughout the organization.

ISO Implementation Is Not a Straight Line

ISO 9000 is not a simple process of going from Point A to Point B in a straight line. While ISO implementation is doable for almost any organization, the way business is conducted may have to be modified if an organization is to comply with ISO requirements. Policies or procedures may have to be radically altered, and changing the way things are done is difficult even in the best of times.

One early adopter of ISO was the Chemical Sector of UCB, a large chemical company in Europe. UCB discovered that two prerequisites must exist before ISO 9000 can be introduced to a company: (1) Management must be committed to the effort and (2) there must be an organizational acceptance and appreciation of the importance of quality. In terms of the first prerequisite, the UCB general manager dovetailed quality objectives and policies into the company's business strategy. In terms of the second prerequisite, once the importance of quality was understood, then an internal quality structure including quality systems could be integrated into the organization.[2]

THE FUTURE OF THE QA DEPARTMENT

What is the responsibility and authority of this QA department many of whose functions have been transferred to everyone in the organization? During ISO adoption and implementation, the QA department also goes through a transition from being a large functional group to being one that is much smaller and higher in the organization. The role of the department changes from performing people-intensive inspection activities to being largely responsible for training, monitoring, and verifying that quality systems are in place and working properly.

During this transition, the quality group continues to provide a valuable contribution to the business. They maintain the quality focus of the organization, serve as an independent authority and evaluator of quality systems, and coordinate among many functions and levels the ongoing process of continuous improvement.

If quality problems arise or staff resources are needed, the quality group may provide inspection, test, or other skills to help the operating personnel solve their own problems. The critical element is that process and system ownership still rests with the workers.

How does the organization or top management know that quality systems are still working? In some cases operational boredom may set in; there may be no nonconformances, deficiencies, corrective actions, or other exceptions to the normal day-to-day operations. The quality department or someone else periodically checks quality systems to affirm that they are still effective and improving.

THE EXPERT'S CORNER
Insights and Tips

This quality system forced us to put specific requirements and guidelines into place for management to use. A checklist was created for the president to make sure all areas of the company were being quality checked. This checklist has also helped employees realize that management is concerned about quality.

EMILY KONOLD,
Q.A. Specialist, Help/Systems

This element of the standard spawned a brainstorming session of the steering committee, which resulted in the restatement of our corporate vision and mission. The realization that Kaizen [continuous improvement] is an element of, and not the driving force behind, our mission brought us to redefine ourselves as "an innovative company," a concept introduced into the quality field in Juran's Management Breakthrough and reaffirmed by Intel's Andy Grove in Quality Forum IX. This executive-level rethinking led to the formulation and deployment of our mission and vision statement and the guiding principles by which our company intends to meet them.

JOHN ZAVACKI,
QA Manager, Suckle Corporation

Don't spend a lot of time and effort until the management of the organization is committed and has gotten involved. We [Kodak Park Division] found that the rate of progress increased significantly once top management of the organization seeking registration became visibly involved through communicating clear expectations, attending (and being a presenter at) ISO training, using every possible opportunity to explain why the organization is seeking registration, and taking an active role in management review meetings.

KAREN LOVECCHIO,
ISO 9000 Coordinator, Kodak Park
Division, Eastman Kodak

We learned the best quality policy is oftentimes the simplest. We had a lengthy quality policy with all the politically acceptable stuff like "enhancing shareholder value." Did the average person coating film relate to that? Were they inspired? Did they understand why they should care about getting ISO 9002 registration? No.

After we got registered in February 1992, we took a collective deep breath and asked, "How do we really want to live with/for our quality system?"

Our ISO core team (a group of reps from all our production and staff areas) decided that the first update—to symbolize simplification and shop-floor ownership—would be a revised quality policy.

Our postregistration quality policy, based on shop-floor feedback, is as follows:

QUALITY POLICY: (THE WHAT)
We manufacture high-quality products and look for ways to do it better.

(continued)

QUALITY PRINCIPLES: (THE HOW)
Customer Focus
Management Leadership
Teamwork
Analytical Approaches
Continuous Improvement

MANAGEMENT REPRESENTATIVE AND VERIFICATION
RESOURCES AND PERSONNEL
We looked at our organization—who had what capabilities—and then decided roles/responsibilities from there. Certainly we've had to make adjustments, but it was very worthwhile at the start of our ISO journey for the management team to do some thinking about resourcing and supporting the people who were given the authority to do internal audits, reviewed releases, etc.

MANAGEMENT REVIEWS
We struggled with how to conduct a meaningful management review of the quality systems covering seven buildings and 1,300-plus people. We started the reviews in July and decided to hold them quarterly. At first, we just focused on preparing for ISO 9002 registration and the results of internal and third-party audits. Eventually our reviews were expanded to cover customer-complaint analysis, corrective-action highlights, and even a quality system health checklist to get the departments to do a "gut" check on four or five of the ISO clauses each month and how they felt their system was adding value to their organization.
                    BETH KRENZER,
                    Manager, Black and White Film
                    Manufacturing, Eastman Kodak

Formal quality policy statements and manuals were developed during each division's ISO program since these were nonexistent prior to ISO implementation. Disseminating the information to all levels of the organization was handled through a variety of publicity techniques including employee badges, posters with employees' signatures, newsletters, etc.

For most divisions, periodic quality performance reviews were already conducted by senior management; therefore, the process only needed to be documented and central files established for record retention.

Our concern under the quality system "management responsibility" dealt with the structure of our organization. Although we had an established quality control system, we did not have traditional quality departments. In our structure, quality is the responsibility of each business unit manager. Basically, each division throughout the entire organization (all employees) is responsible for quality, with the division director or vice president ultimately responsible. The ISO coordinator/audit manager reports directly to this manager. This enables direct communication of quality system breakdowns.

> JOANNE MAYO,
> Corporate ISO Coordinator,
> Data General

The advantage of this quality system is that the entire company remains focused on the purpose of the business and continuous improvement. Management stays involved at all levels of the quality system process.

> DARYL PARKER,
> Director, A.G.A. Quality,
> ISO Registrar

Management must be aware of, and have an understanding of, what quality is and their role in the quality process. This requirement is tested by the registrar by interviewing several people throughout a given plant to determine whether management is fully behind the process. The system also cannot punish people who bring quality problems to the attention of management.

Management must also have the right attitude toward quality. They must give their full support to accomplishing the firm's quality objectives, providing the necessary resources, and showing their commitment to working under the defined quality systems (i.e., by performing management reviews and participating in indoctrination and training).

Management policy must be written in terms of measurable objectives.

(continued)

The firm's employees should know how their jobs affect quality. The employees should be able to communicate the quality policy to the assessment team.

Management has to place the appropriate personnel in the jobs necessary to produce a quality product. This means individuals can stop nonconforming product themselves or take the necessary actions to start the process to correct the problem.

Management must appoint someone with the responsibility to ensure that the requirements of the standard are met. That individual must have adequate knowledge of the ISO 9000 standard so he or she can assess compliance, and must have the authority to implement the standard. A production manager could be the representative, but his or her quality-related tasks must be clear.

Frequent management reviews should be performed at appropriate intervals, which should be based on such factors as market changes and the maturity of the supplier's quality system. The review should be used as an internal feedback loop for improvement.

ANDREW BERGMAN,
Manager of Certification,
OTS Quality Registrars

4.2

Quality Systems

While systems are important, our main reliance must always be put on men rather than on systems.

ROBERT E. WOOD,
CEO, Sears Roebuck

QUICK SCAN
ISO 9001 Requirements

Quality systems are maintained and documented throughout the organization to assure external and internal customer satisfaction. The quality system is documented through a quality manual, procedures, and workmanship standards.

The quality system must ensure operational consistency. Quality plans are the means to define how quality system requirements are met in a contract, and outline the specific sequence of activities necessary to satisfy contract requirements.

WHAT ARE QUALITY SYSTEMS?

Quality systems are the fundamental component of ISO 9000. ISO standard 8402 defines a quality system as "the organizational structure, responsibilities, procedures, processes, and resources needed to implement quality management.[1] There are 20 key quality systems in ISO 9001, from management responsibility to document control to corrective action to statistical techniques. Systems and process thinking is fundamental to any quality initiative. A central tenet is that everything in an organization is linked and is part of a process. A number of processes can comprise a system, and systems form the operational backbone of the organization. A process can be composed of machines, methods, communication, documentation, employees, policies, leadership, organizational culture, and attitudes. In this holistic view, no event is isolated and no process stands alone.

QUALITY SYSTEM CONTROL

Quality system controls are documentation-intensive. Documentation is evidence to management or an outside authority such as the registrar that a company understands customer requirements and has established quality system procedures and instructions to satisfy these requirements.

An organization's quality systems are documented through a hierarchy of quality documentation. Each progressive tier of documentation becomes more detailed and specific. Quality documentation follows the previously discussed three-level hierarchy of quality manual, procedures, and work instructions. Quality system documentation may also include:

• Test and inspection instructions.

• Quality standards.

• Quality specifications.

• Engineering drawings.

HOW TO ESTABLISH QUALITY SYSTEMS

The quality system concept incorporates all the organizational elements to define, monitor, control, and improve quality. The process of establishing a quality system starts with identifying customer requirements, then defining strategies, policies, procedures, and work instructions so requirements can be satisfied throughout the organization. This process follows a straightforward path of:

- Identifying customer requirements.
- Identifying process variables and product characteristics.
- Developing organizational quality requirements.
- Developing quality plans on how quality can be verified.
- Acquiring manufacturing processes, quality controls, inspection equipment, methods, personnel, and fixtures.
- Acquiring production, test, and measurement equipment to maintain production capability.
- Aligning design, testing, production, and installation processes.
- Establishing quality records systems.
- Satisfying regulatory requirements.

CHANGING HABITS AND OPERATIONS

Quality systems should be structured so that they can be used for decision making. Otherwise, they exist only on paper and in procedures but are not used. The following examples may illustrate the importance of this point: Training systems are developed by trainers who don't know how employees do their jobs; corrective action system procedures stipulate that quality staff, instead of line personnel, are responsible for corrective action.

If system procedures are not followed, then they should be changed. However, people often resist change until the logic of the change that is needed is clearly understood and is not threatening. One option is to give employees information when a problem arises and let them take action based on the data. Information can be collected through several means, including inspection, statistical process control, or fishbone diagrams. The data can then be used to arrive at a consensus as to the cause of the problem and the recommended action.

THE EXPERT'S CORNER
Insights and Tips

The quality manual becomes a lifesaver for new employees. Since we put this in place, every new employee has commented on how helpful it has been in terms of understanding responsibilities.
EMILY KONOLD,
Q. A. Specialist, Help/Systems

We followed a systems analytic approach to ISO implementation. This approach aided us in implementing management review and internal quality audits. By analyzing our quality systems in a disciplined and rigorous manner, we began understanding and identifying system flaws more rapidly.

The benefits of using this system are many. When the entire organization is involved in its redesign, people begin to understand the nature of a system and the impact of individual action on its diverse elements. ISO implementation efforts have assisted us in implementing our concurrent effort of installing an enterprise information system. The organizational dynamic has gone from adaptive to genera-

tive learning during the process. Team thinking and cross-functional problem solving have become common elements of our business processes.
                                                JOHN ZAVACKI,
                                                QA Manager, Suckle Corporation

We first read the ISO 9000 standards in 1990 and thought this clause was difficult to understand because it seemed to be saying what we thought the entire standard was about. Our core team eventually developed the documentation structure and linkages to give all our areas guidance on how the quality systems should be linked. We debated the merits of centralized versus decentralized quality systems to the nth degree. We ended up with an overall, fairly generic quality manual, and local master quality reference documents guiding all the departments on the "what" but not the "how to" of the standard's clauses. And, of course, procedures and work instructions made up the base of our documentation structure. We decided early on to keep the administration simple since ISO did require so much effort to document all our practices/procedures and to close holes in all our practices.
                                                BETH KRENZER,
                                                Manager, Black and White Film
                                                Manufacturing, Eastman Kodak

The primary reason Data General has been so successful with each ISO implementation phase has been because of the existing quality system. For most divisions, the system already met 80 percent to 90 percent of the ISO requirements, but was not completely documented. Preparation for ISO required review of existing procedures and work instructions, many of which were no longer valid. This lead to a large reduction in the number of documented instructions. The remaining were revised to reflect current practices and only a small portion were created to meet the ISO requirements that were not in place (ie: Internal Audits, training records, etc.).
                                                JOANNE MAYO,
                                                Corporate ISO Coordinator,
                                                Data General

(continued)

A thoroughly and appropriately documented system provides continuity of purpose and a road map for providing a quality product. This results in less waste in terms of time and materials.

DARYL PARKER,
Director, A.G.A. Quality,
ISO Registrar

The company must have the necessary documentation to control all the supporting elements in the 9001 standards. When auditing a quality system for implementation, each company will have a different view on what needs to be included. It is the job of the ISO assessment team to make sure the level of documentation is sufficient for ensuring a quality product.

ANDREW BERGMAN,
Manager of Certification,
OTS Quality Registrars

4.3

Contract Review

QUICK SCAN
ISO 9001 Requirements

Customer requirements are reviewed prior to and while the contract is in force. Process, product, delivery, quality, cost, and other factors are defined and understood. New or modified products and new contracts are formally reviewed in order to satisfy customer requirements.

LISTENING TO THE CUSTOMER

Companies are focusing on the customer and the marketplace to drive their quality efforts. Listening to the customer is part of every company's strategy. Companies are focusing on their core competencies and aligning their efforts to the new marketplace. For example, Alcoa has listened to its customers and has realigned to focus on its core aluminum business. To understand customer requirements, Alcoa formed interdisciplinary customer listening teams, consisting of sales, marketing, engineering, and production personnel.[1]

Poor quality has often resulted from misunderstandings between customer and supplier. To avert this, customer requirements must be thoroughly spelled out in contractual boilerplate, engineering drawings, bills of material, testing requirements, and other technical documents.

An important mechanism that can be used to listen to customers is contract review. Contract review is the process prior to and after the contract is signed to determine whether the supplier understands and can comply with the contract requirements. Customer requirements are spelled out in a contract or purchase order. To facilitate understanding and compliance, suppliers are expected to review all contracts.

A contract specifies terms and conditions the customer requires the supplier to meet. These requirements may address all or part of the following:

- *Test requirements* entail special testing, inspection, and measurement instructions.

- *Product specifications* detail functional, fit, structural, or chemical requirements for critical product attributes.

- *Process specifications* include control and capability requirements for critical process variables.

- *Production capabilities* specify the number of products to be produced within set time periods.

- *Delivery requirements* spell out sequence, packaging, labeling, handling, storage, or transportation requirements.

HOW ARE CONTRACTS CONTROLLED?

This quality system specifically requires suppliers to establish and maintain contract review procedures. However, the customer— the purchaser—also has requirements not addressed in the specification that are just as important. If the customer doesn't know what he or she wants and doesn't spell this out in the contract documents, then disappointment often follows.

Contract review may involve some or all of the following steps:

- Customer requirements are fully defined.
- Suppliers fully understand contract requirements.
- Suppliers are able to meet customer requirements.
- Suppliers prepare a plan for implementing the contract.
- Contract compliance is continuously monitored.

THE EXPERT'S CORNER
Insights and Tips

I misinterpreted the contract review quality system at first. I figured something had to be signed to institute a contract, but found this requirement was anything that constituted an agreement with the user of the product in terms of what it would do or how it would do it.

EMILY KONOLD,
Q.A. Specialist, Help/Systems

Contract review made us look at our customer's requirements quite differently. At first we did not consider a product request as a contract or one that required review. But it did.

DAVID BALLARD, quality consultant

Black and White Film Manufacturing produces X-ray, graphic arts, motion picture, and professional black-and-white films primarily to stock order. We have a decent MRP II system to assure we communicate with our marketing and sales partners. For ISO 9002, we had to think about how we document this process. We used records of our demand and operational meeting notes as evidence that we were meeting "contracts." The key to this clause is to do what makes the most sense for your customer, then document and track its progress.

BETH KRENZER,
Manager, Black and White Film
Manufacturing, Eastman Kodak

(continued)

The majority of Data General sales consist of predefined products and services which are cataloged as standard, although customers may request products/services that are unique. In either case, the requirements of the customer are documented on-line for internal use and in a contract. Applicable divisions have defined responsibilities for reviewing the non-standard requests and determining the capability of meeting the requirements.

> JOANNE MAYO,
> Corporate ISO Coordinator,
> Data General

By implementing this quality requirement, interface among the sub-contractor, supplier, and the customer is enhanced, thus leading to a better product.

> DARYL PARKER,
> Director, A.G.A. Quality,
> ISO Registrar

Oftentimes in a small company, especially one with very specific expertise in a given target market (e.g., the drilling of deep, offshore gas wells), the supplier must bring its expertise to the review of the contract to make sure the customer's requirements have been adequately defined. Often the supplier will be more knowledgeable than the customer about the specific field they do work in. If the supplier can assist and educate the customer, the customer will value the supplier's contribution.

So it's critical that the supplier has the ability to adequately understand customers' needs. If the supplier does not provide adequate specifications, the customer must be able to adequately ascertain that the requirements are based on their experience. The supplier should involve many different departments, and there must be effective communication throughout the process.

> ANDREW BERGMAN,
> Manager of Certification,
> OTS Quality Registrars

4.4

Design Control

One of the only ways to compete is with technology.
JOHN H. BEAKES,
RWD Technologies

QUICK SCAN
ISO 9001 Requirements

Quality elements, such as safety, performance, and dependability, are defined and controlled throughout product development. Product design input and output information is reviewed, verified, documented, and communicated to the appropriate parties.

Product design input requirements, such as performance specifications, configuration composition, materials, process data, and others, are identified and documented.

Product design output requirements, such as process requirements, acceptance criteria, test information, environmental requirements, and others, are documented in drawings, specifications, instructions, or other quality documentation.

Designs are planned, verified, and controlled through design reviews, qualification tests, calculations, or comparisons with proven designs.

Design modifications are monitored, controlled, verified, and documented through an approved document control procedure.

WHAT IS GOOD DESIGN?

For functional, aesthetic, and manufacturable design, the simplest configurations often work best. Complicated configurations—for example, thin-wall sections or complex contours—magnify tooling and manufacturing problems, resulting in a rise in costs. While there are many universal laws for good design, the following are some important rules of thumb:

- Design is reviewed continuously by the development team.
- Design incorporates a minimum number of parts.
- Parts are defect free.
- Design has a suitable safety margin.
- Design incorporates parallel circuits for redundancy.
- Design is manufacturable and testable.
- Design is modularized as much as possible.
- Subassemblies are minimized.
- Design is tested.
- Design emphasizes standardization for new or existing models.
- Engineering changes are documented and authorized by appropriate personnel.

SIMULTANEOUS PRODUCT DEVELOPMENT

Product development has radically changed in the last five years. Quality, multidisciplinary teams, and simultaneous development have emerged as critical product development issues. Zero defects can only be assured at the design stage. Responsibility has shifted from designing components to developing subassemblies or assemblies by integrated product development teams. Probably the most critical element of product design has been simultaneous or concurrent engineering. The new focus is on simultaneous development incorporating input from all those who can contribute, including Manufacturing and suppliers.

Product design used to be a linear effort. Marketing determined customer needs and developed a product brief. Engineering designed the product. Purchasing secured suppliers to provide components and assemblies. Manufacturing produced and assembled the product. Quality Assurance inspected and tested the product. Marketing sold the product. And Distribution sent the product to the customer. This linear process was long and complicated.

In concurrent—or, as it is sometimes called, simultaneous—engineering, a multidisciplinary team develops the product in unison. The goal is to reduce the development cycle and be the first to bring a product to market. Delays and costs associated with rework, engineering modifications, or change orders are avoided.

WHAT IS DESIGN REVIEW?

Design review is a continuous effort by the multidisciplinary team to review each element of product development before it is sent to Manufacturing or to suppliers. During design review, the customer and supplier meet to evaluate documentation, specifications, standards, directions, and other critical information that hopefully will eliminate changes during production. At a minimum, effective design review ensures that resources are available during production, suppliers are chosen carefully, and the design is producible.[1] Design review is conducted at each major milestone or stage of a design, and is multidisciplinary, incorporating the comments and required approvals of all parties involved.

Design development starts with understanding customer requirements. These are detailed in a document called a product brief. Design criteria, including benchmarks, approvals, and acceptance criteria, are spelled out in the brief, then detailed technical specifications for materials, assemblies, components, and manufacturing processes are developed. The product brief, design, and specifications have to be manufacturable, controllable, and verifiable throughout the product development process.

Stages in Product Development

Product development or design goes through the following steps:

1. Wants, needs, and expectations identification stage

   • Identify potential customers.

   • List and prioritize critical needs of each target group.

   • Identify tangible and intangible product characteristics.

   • Identify environmental, regulatory, and cost constraints to using the product.

2. Conceptual stage

   • Study applicable technologies.

   • Examine competing products.

   • Determine design constraints.

   • Account for global marketing.

   • Consider timing.

3. Product design stage

   • Develop preliminary design.

   • Determine prototype construction.

   • Control and assure design integrity.

   • Optimize design.

   • Conduct product testing.

   • Conduct trial production run.

4. Test-marketing assessment stage

   • Alter quality characteristics, if required.

   • Redesign packaging.

   • Modify or update brand or label.

   • Add product value.

   • Modify product line.

HOW ARE DESIGNS CONTROLLED?

Design control is one of the hallmark quality system requirements of ISO 9001. The supplier must verify that a product's design meets customers' requirements. Design is where the highest probability of error rests. A deficient design can replicate its error in each product.

Quality requirements in a design include elements such as performance, safety, labels, packaging, dependability, and maintenance. These product characteristics are sometimes identified as critical, major, and minor, specifying their relative quality level and importance to the customer. The following paragraphs illustrate important design controls.

Design and Development Planning

Procedures are developed for managing a design project, including developing schedules, assigning accountability, evaluating performance, establishing time lines, identifying critical project milestones, identifying resources, planning project goals, and verifying completion.

Activity Assignment

Design review at each stage of product development is often assigned to specific parties. Manufacturing and production personnel evaluate the design for producibility. Quality personnel evaluate reliability and maintainability. Purchasing and quality personnel work with suppliers to assure compatibility of the sourced products.

Organizational and Technical Interfaces

Suppliers and subsuppliers are a critical part of the value-adding supplier chain. Interfacing with outside suppliers is especially important as the amount of outsourced materials increases. Interface control is critical down the supplier chain in order to guarantee that assemblies, subassemblies, and components satisfy the technical requirements of the entire project. Critical design project activities are identified and key personnel are selected to complete the activities throughout the value-adding chain.

Design Input

Design input is solicited from many external and internal groups, including Research/Development, suppliers, Engineering, Field Service, and others. The input is then integrated into the product or service.

Design input disagreements and conflicts are resolved as quickly as possible. Present or future project or product difficulties are also anticipated.

Design Output

The design process results in outputs, including bills of material, performance specifications, drawings, and many others. Outputs are reviewed and verified to confirm accuracy, coherence, completeness, understandability, and customer satisfaction.

Design Verification

Four design controls include qualification tests, recalculations, comparisons with proven designs, and design reviews. Design review is probably the most common design verification tool.

Design Changes

Designs may be modified as a result of market changes, errors, testing results, safety reasons, and corrective-action changes. Modifications have to be accurately reflected in all documentation, drawings, and other design documentation.

Tools and techniques used in design review include:

- Design control procedures.
- Multidisciplinary teams.
- Design of experiments.
- Feasibility studies.
- Value engineering.
- Design-for-manufacturability procedures.
- Taguchi studies.

- Geometric Design and Tolerancing.

- Engineering change orders.

- Part number and/or specification updates.

THE EXPERT'S CORNER
Insights and Tips

Design control forced us to be specific in our software design requirements—i.e., exact fields to be in files and exact information required on screens (even positioning concerns). It helped our programmers know instead of guess.

EMILY KONOLD,
Q.A. Specialist, Help/Systems

Products and services are typically designed to address a wide variety of customer needs. The design input is driven by current technology capabilities, rather than by a specific customer.

Software design control encompasses the full software development process. Requirements are established for each release, on which schedules and plans are based. Design reviews, code reviews, and testing are used to ensure that the finished software meets the defined requirements. Design changes are tracked throughout the process by updating design documents as the design is changed.

Within Systems Development, the implementation of the ISO program progressed differently than in the manufacturing and service divisions. Few repetitive processes were in place, and none were documented. The first step was to document what each engineering specialty department contributed to the development of a new product, and their internal processes for identifying product requirements, verifying product acceptability, and preparing their piece of the product for production. The major challenge in this division's implementation came next, in defining the critical hand-offs between departments, and the processes for defining, managing, tracking, and accountability of those hand-offs. Prior to ISO implementation, these processes were determined independently by each project manager. Today, the process is broken into five phases, each with defined activities, deliverables, and an executive phase exit review that provides project visibility and accountability.

> JOANNE MAYO,
> Corporate ISO Coordinator,
> Data General

A thorough system of control provides a basis for identifying opportunities for improvement and prevention of nonconformances. Enhancement of the product and development of new products is thus possible. The customer satisfaction level is increased and both customer and supplier (subcontractor) benefit.

> DARYL PARKER,
> Director, A.G.A. Quality,
> ISO Registrar

The company must adequately define responsibilities for its design activities. The organizational and technical interfaces shall be identified. Existing designs must still meet the requirements of this standard.

One way for firms to identify the important input factors in their design is to have a "critical components list." If this exists, there should be additional justification for how these critical components are handled in their processes (i.e., additional receiving inspection, etc.).

> ANDREW BERGMAN,
> Manager of Certification,
> OTS Quality Registrars

4.5

Document Control

A computer won't clean up the errors in your manual of procedures.
SHEILA M. EBY, business writer

QUICK SCAN
ISO 9001 Requirements

Complete, accurate, and usable quality system documents are developed and controlled. Responsibilities for issuance, distribution, and approval are detailed in procedures.

Preparation, handling, approval, recording, and distribution of changes to documents are also detailed.

INCREASING IMPORTANCE OF DOCUMENTS

Competitive information is used to secure markets and generate profits. Proprietary data is among the most important competitive information a company has. Companies are very serious about safeguarding this information.

The challenge is that all company personnel need to be provided with current and accurate information so they can make quality decisions. Current and accurate quality documentation is important for design verification. Customers, regulatory authorities, or internal groups require quality documentation to verify that actions were completed, directions followed, requirements met, tests conducted, problems solved, design requirements met, processes are stable, or for a number of other reasons.

WHAT IS DOCUMENT CONTROL?

A quality management program involves extensive and intensive documentation and records management. Some have called ISO requirements a living organism that develops and cares for documents from conception and generation through disposition. In most cases, a wide variety of documentation is involved. For example, a set of engineering drawings of a product can include a bill of materials, multiple product views, different levels of detail, assembly instructions, and test requirements. This bundle of information must be accurate, precise, approved, current, and comprehensive. An effective document control system confirms that these objectives are attained.

The value of a documentation control system can be appreciated when a design is modified. Product drawings must be revised so information continues to be accurate throughout multiple product changes. First, baseline documentation is collected for a new design and may consist of bills of material, production standards, quality specifications, inspection requirements, and engineering prints. If the design should change for some reason—even if it's a small part from a supplier three tiers removed—the change must be reflected in the current set of design documentation. Working files are also updated and approved by the appropriate parties.[1]

An effective documentation control system also minimizes risks and exposure to litigation. If a company has documented quality system controls, sufficient product testing, and other quality-control measures, then it can affect the outcome of a case.

HOW ARE DOCUMENTS CONTROLLED?

The essential element of document control, which involves critical documents within the quality system extending into the suppliers' quality systems is to define what is controlled, who is responsible for the control, and how it will be controlled.

Document Approval and Issuance

Document control implies that the initiation, development, distribution, revision, and termination of documents are defined and procedures are consistently followed. At initiation, all relevant personnel are consulted for input into the design process. During development, documents are dated, reviewed, identified, secured, and approved at each step of the process. As documents are distributed, they are made accessible to all qualified personnel. During revision, document changes are also dated, reviewed, and approved. At termination, they are removed from service.

Document Changes/Modifications

Document changes and modifications are especially susceptible to quality degradation. In large organizations, many departments can issue documents and approve changes, so it's critical that current and accurate documents are used throughout the system. Employees are then aware of the most current or revised document. Random audits are conducted to verify that current drawings and documentation are used. Also, access to critical or proprietary records is controlled. Quality documents are controlled by assigning control responsibility, reviewing authority, developing revision procedures, and specifying locations of documents. The control process often starts with a master list of documents and revisions. Each time a new document is issued or a change is approved, the change is recorded in the master document list. At a minimum, records are legible, dated, clean, identifiable, comprehensive, and current.

The list of quality documents to be controlled is extensive. Some of the more important ones include:

- Quality standards
- Technical specifications
- Industry standards
- Policies
- Work procedures
- Work instructions
- Engineering prints
- Inspection reports
- Quality manual
- Test data
- Calibration data
- Material review reports
- Bills of material
- Audit reports

PAPERLESS DOCUMENTATION

More manufacturing and service organizations are using computers to store, collate, analyze, and retrieve information. In plants with multiple production lines, many different model numbers, and many suppliers, the amount of paperwork increases exponentially. For this reason, many companies are choosing paperless quality system documentation. For example, electronic gauges and on-line process control may inspect 100 or more points on the production line. Because manual tracking of this information is a nightmare, the solution is to test, measure, control and document results electronically.

THE EXPERT'S CORNER
Insights and Tips

If I were to say we have a problem area, developing documentation would be it. We have an easy-to-use quality manual. When changes need to be made, a cover sheet accompanies the order, showing all the necessary changes. Some employees are careful and update the information well. Some employees are not. We are looking into an on-line document-handling system, but until then we end up doing a lot of manual checks.
EMILY KONOLD,
Q.A. Specialist, Help/Systems

This element is key and still causes the most noncompliance in our ongoing internal/external audits. You can find good electronic document control systems (mainframe or PC) or you can make your paperwork system work well. The key is teamwork on the part of the users of the system. It is their system, and the more they are involved in updating, reviewing, and controlling documents, the less likely the system will fall apart or get bypassed.

We tend to use a two-column format for most of our procedures. The left-hand column identifies the key steps in a procedure, while the right column gives more detail and background for those with a need or desire to know more.
BETH KRENZER,
Manager, Black and White Film
Manufacturing, Eastman Kodak

Documentation Control is an area where most companies do not succeed on their first assessment, especially large companies where automation

(continued)

does not exist. This is a strong area for Data General. Most documentation is maintained on-line where all employees can retrieve policies, procedures, work instructions, and engineering changes directly from their workstations. Data General has the capability to access policies and procedures from facilities around the world. This has enabled organizations to share information, particularly during the development of ISO programs. The software tools used are products Data General markets and sells, primarily "CEO", Comprehensive Electronic Office, and UNIX based packages. Having the latest information readily available electronically for all levels of employees eliminates issues relating to control of obsolete documentation and hard copy distribution. Changes are transmitted on a real-time basis. This ensures all team members are playing the game by the same rules.

JOANNE MAYO,
Corporate ISO Coordinator,
Data General

An appropriate documentation control system must thread throughout the organization. This provides the foundation for operational efficiency and control.

DARYL PARKER,
Director, A.G.A. Quality,
ISO Registrar

Any instruction controlling quality activities must be approved and reviewed by management. Examples of these are software, external standards, forms, equipment, method of document transmittal, approval, distribution, and master list. A table of contents is often the most widely used method for having a "master list" of documents

ANDREW BERGMAN,
Manager of Certification,
OTS Quality Registrars

4.6

Purchasing

QUICK SCAN
ISO 9001 Requirements

Purchasing is planned and controlled through specifications, performance monitoring, inspection, feedback systems, reliability testing, and site audits.

Suppliers can be assessed through product testing, evaluation by a third party (such as a registrar), or a customer-supplier audit. Criteria to be assessed include quality, cost, technology, delivery, and service.

A PRODUCT IS ONLY AS RELIABLE AS ITS COMPONENTS

Companies look to suppliers to control the quality of incoming goods, implement just-in-time delivery, and eliminate incoming material inspection. Companies increasingly audit suppliers, certify them, and expect zero-defect levels. If suppliers comply, rewards are shared. Suppliers are likely to get larger and longer-term contracts, technical assistance, and special equipment.

In this changing relationship, Purchasing's role is less that of a department whose mission is mainly to procure products and material at the lowest price to one of procuring products while optimizing quality, service, availability, and price.

All purchased material, parts, and assemblies conform to specifications, blueprints, and/or industry standards. In addition, products must be competitively priced, delivered on time, available as needed, and innovative. These factors are usually spelled out in a contract or purchase order.

As the primary link with suppliers, the Purchasing and Quality departments review dimensional specifications with suppliers to certify that sizes, weights, and tolerances are exactly what is required to make the product. Questions about the appropriateness, tightness, and looseness of the specifications are also discussed with the supplier's and customer's engineering representatives. This is important because specifications of complex equipment can run many pages and can include quality requirements that second-, third-, and even fourth-tier suppliers must conform to.

In selecting a supplier, Purchasing plans, coordinates, and consults with Engineering, Quality, and Manufacturing. Engineering supplies the material specifications of what should be purchased. Quality audits suppliers to determine whether they can manufacture products to meet specifications. And Manufacturing supplies feedback on any changes that may be required of the supplier.

HOW ARE PURCHASED MATERIALS CONTROLLED?

The purchase of supplies must be planned and controlled if they are to conform to customer requirements. This requires a close working relationship with suppliers, mutually understood requirements, and a rapid feedback system to resolve differences. The goal is to verify that customer and supplier understand each other's requirements. Conveying information is an interactive process. Information is communicated verbally and through documents.

What Makes a "World Class" Supplier?

Companies are selecting "world class" suppliers. What makes for one? The following are considered "world class" supplier requirements:

• Desire for a long-term relationship.

• Financial stability.

• Inventory management and control mechanisms.

• Clean facilities.

• High automation level.

• Advanced quality techniques employed in QC.

• State-of-the-art research and development activities.

• Recent investments in plant and equipment.

• Management progressiveness to try new methods.

• Willingness to share costs with the customer.

Procurement follows a cycle that starts with selecting a supplier and ends with establishing a partnering relationship with a supplier. The procurement lifecycle begins in the product development stage of the development cycle. In this stage, the development team, which includes representatives from Purchasing, looks for possible product or service providers. As a product changes through the product lifecycle, alterations in design or specifications are communicated to suppliers.

General Systems

Customers follow a process of selecting, monitoring, and improving suppliers. The first step to ensuring that purchased products conform to requirements is determining whether the customer and supplier speak a common language and understand each other's requirements. The customer must develop clear and accurate engineering drawings, specifications, contracts, manufacturing plans, and other instructions.

Purchasing Data

Often the customer-supplier communication process starts with a broad document that specifies customer requirements, including quality, technology, service, cost, and delivery. More specific information may include physical composition, performance requirements, inspection methods, packaging/labeling information, manufacturing requirements, regulatory specifications, inspection instructions, reliability requirements, system registration mandates, and so forth.

Assessment of Subcontractors

Suppliers are also responsible for selecting and monitoring subcontractors—the supplier's suppliers—in the same manner that they are selected and monitored. Subcontractors (also known as subsuppliers) are expected to consistently meet product and service requirements at the lowest cost, and supply defect-free products just-in-time as they are to be used.

This process extends into the supplier base. Suppliers or subcontractors are expected to also consistently meet the supplier's requirements as well as the customer's. These subsuppliers may be audited by the customer, have their products tested, or have their quality systems ISO registered. Customer-imposed requirements are being pushed down the supplier chain as the customers expect to work only with "approved" suppliers throughout the value-adding process.

Verification of Purchased Products

Some products or components pose a higher risk than others, so the customer may require additional testing or other types of assurance, or may even want to verify the purchased products personally. This can mean a visit to the supplier's facility or testing incoming products. Inspection or testing can extend to the sub-supplier facility. When this level of assurance extends to the supplier, requirements must be spelled out in the contract. Responsibility for quality cannot be absolved and still rests with the source. The supplier is responsible for its quality and so on down the supplier chain.

THE EXPERT'S CORNER
Insights and Tips

This quality system helped us in terms of setting up guidelines for hiring contractor software-testing personnel.
EMILY KONOLD,
Q.A. Specialist, Help/Systems

We did a lot of thinking about how we would put together our approved supplier list. In some cases we used historical performance indicators, in others incoming inspection and subcontractor audits. Many of our subcontractors were internal to Kodak. Of course, we asked them to get registered, but in the meanwhile we wrote interface agreements specifying our requirements, and we also did assessments of these subcontractors periodically.
BETH KRENZER,
Manager, Black and White Film
Manufacturing, Eastman Kodak

During the design stage, suppliers for required materials are assessed to verify their ability to meet product specifications, to provide sufficient quantities in a timely manner, and to produce at acceptable quality levels for a reasonable cost. Within the servicing arena, suppliers can be used when multiple types/brands of equipment are placed under the same service contract. Upon qualification, these suppliers are placed on an "approved vendor list." Continual assessment of supplier performance is

(continued)

conducted by each division. Unacceptable performance is reported to the vendor. Inability to meet the established agreements may be cause for revocation of approved vendor status. Alternate suppliers are qualified using the same methods.

> JOANNE MAYO,
> Corporate ISO Coordinator,
> Data General

Effective and efficient control of purchases can reduce a company's operating costs. Implementing this quality system improves communication between the subcontractor and the customer.

> DARYL PARKER,
> Director, A.G.A. Quality,
> ISO Registrar

A company should establish a feedback system with its vendors to ensure that continuous improvement is occurring and that the relationship is not just a "club" to beat vendors over the head with.

A company should have sufficient quality records to demonstrate the ability of contractors and subcontractors to meet specified requirements. However, the supplier should also consider, where applicable, the technical capabilities of the vendors and simply not accept vendors on the sole basis that they're ISO 9000 certified.

Supplier history must be used with caution. The supplier's decision to use a vendor must be based on current, objective evidence to support the history.

The revision status of documents referenced in the purchase order should be accurate, and any referenced specifications must be thoroughly identified. Purchasing documents should have revision numbers also referenced on the purchase order to indicate the revision level of the purchase order.

The company should use information gained from the vendor to determine the best method to verify the purchased product.

> ANDREW BERGMAN,
> Manager of Certification,
> OTS Quality Registrars

4.7

Purchaser-Supplied Products

QUICK SCAN
ISO 9001 Requirements

The supplier shall identify, count, and inspect supplied materials, as well as verify that they conform to contract and quality requirements. If supplied products are damaged or lost, the customer will be immediately notified.

GROWING IMPORTANCE OF
PURCHASER-SUPPLIED PRODUCTS

Most companies are focusing on what they do well and sourcing more work to suppliers. As customers outsource more work to suppliers, accurate communication becomes critical. The customer must explicitly communicate its requirements to the supplier, and the supplier has to understand what the customer wants and be able to comply. Often communication can get bogged down because of poor understanding, poor equipment, and poor specifications.

Sometimes the customer may require special handling, testing, or other elements above and beyond the normal course of business. In these cases, the customer provides the supplier with

equipment it owns. Purchaser-supplied products are those owned
by the purchaser, who provides them to the supplier to meet its
special requirements.

As the links between customer and supplier become closer, the
supplier may be asked to assemble a special product or conduct
special tests. For example, the customer may ask the supplier to
fabricate special jigs, fixtures, or additional production equipment. The customer may require the supplier to test or manufacture products in a specific fashion. This equipment is specially
designed to measure very close tolerances. Or the customer may
require the supplier to conduct nondestructive testing or on-line
ultrasound inspection, or transport radioactive material in pro-
tective containers. Or the customer may require the supplier to
add customer proprietary materials to the supplier's chemical
process.

Whatever the customer request, the supplier is ultimately responsible for installing the control systems for these tests, transporting radioactive materials, or complying with the contract. So
the customer, or purchaser, may provide raw material, containers,
packaging, or inspection equipment. The purchaser may also
provide services, such as transportation or inspectors.

HOW ARE PURCHASER-SUPPLIED PRODUCTS CONTROLLED?

In this relationship, the purchaser and the supplier both have
special responsibilities for ensuring quality. The purchaser must
provide information or resources that will mesh with those of the
supplier. For example, the purchaser is responsible for assuring
that the test equipment is compatible with that of the supplier, or
for ensuring that its personnel are knowledgeable of the supplier's
capabilities.

The customer is responsible for:

- Communicating requirements to the supplier.

- Explaining how to use the loaned equipment.

- Providing acceptable materials and/or services.

- Explaining transportation, handling, and packaging instructions to the supplier.

And the supplier is responsible for:

- Treating equipment as its own.

- Identifying, maintaining, and storing equipment so it is not damaged.

- Complying with and understanding customer requirements.

- Verifying quantities and quality of supplied materials.

- Examining supplied materials and equipment to determine any transportation or handling damage.

- Examining materials periodically during storage to prevent deterioration.

- Maintaining records of traceability and quality of materials of supplied materials.

- Returning materials not used or equipment already used.

THE EXPERT'S CORNER
Insights and Tips

Black and White Film Manufacturing does not normally use purchaser-supplied products. Our quality manual states that no purchaser-supplied product is incorporated in our products. In the event that

(continued)

purchaser-supplied products were *received, a procedure would be written to provide for verification, storage, and maintenance for the products.*
> BETH KRENZER,
> Manager, Black and White Film
> Manufacturing, Eastman Kodak

Normally when a customer places an order it is composed of materials manufactured or provided by Data General. On occasion, the customer may require the inclusion or integration of unique material or the addition of a service not normally provided by Data General. For example, a value added reseller (VAR) may want a specific software package installed on a computer system or the customer may wish to have our competitor's products also serviced. Data General's processes are flexible enough to handle these exceptions. Documented instructions ensure proper controls are maintained.
> JOANNE MAYO,
> Corporate ISO Coordinator,
> Data General

A system of control can reduce costs and prevent problems. It improves the image of the company in the eyes of the customer.
> DARYL PARKER,
> Director, A.G.A. Quality,
> ISO Registrar

The supplier accepts responsibility for prevention from damage, for identification, maintenance, storage, and handling. The customer should arrange for the following:

- *Examination of the product upon receipt.*

- *Periodic inspections to confirm proper condition.*

- *Compliance with any contract requirements for reinspection.*

- *Prevention against unauthorized use.*
> ANDREW BERGMAN,
> Manager of Certification,
> OTS Quality Registrars

4.8

Product Identification and Traceability

QUICK SCAN
ISO 9001 Requirements

Procedures are established to identify and document materials and products used throughout the product development and product lifecycles. In-house and supplied materials are traceable. If spelled out in a contract, products or shipments are uniquely identifiable and traceable.

WHY ARE PRODUCT IDENTIFICATION AND TRACEABILITY IMPORTANT?

Product identification and traceability are important quality systems for problem solving, quality improvement, or product recall. Product identification is the means of identifying one product from another. Product traceability is the record and documentation, on an engineering print or bill of materials, of one or a batch of products from origin through customer receipt and use.

With product identification and traceability, if a part is out of

"We've Got to Use the Material"

In any production person's career, there is a time when unverified supplied products are used. The reasons for the urgency vary. The customer wants products quickly. Production downtime is very expensive. Past shipments have been approved and use of this shipment poses little risk. There is an administrative error and the certifications will be supplied tomorrow. Whatever the reason for using the materials, products should be positively identified. That way, if they are deficient, they can be identified, segregated, and recalled efficiently.

A critical element of quality control is verifying that all processes are consistent. If for some reason nonconforming products from a supplier are used or released before quality inspection is complete, products are traceable. Issuing waivers or deviations is frowned upon. Consistency is subordinated to get the product out the door or for some other expedient reason. It is essential that there be total traceability of these nonconforming products. Products should be released only if the materials can be identified, so if a problem should arise, products can be segregated and corrective action can be conducted.

spec, the operator can identify when the problem occurred and determine the cause. It's important to positively identify a shipment, batch, or group of products so products go to the right location, the source of products is identified, and the test/inspection status is clear. If there is a product recall, product identification allows all products to be retrieved. If similar products become commingled, it's possible to separate them by grade. If multiple shipments of similar products arrive, it's possible to identify the source of the nonconforming products.

Why is traceability important? Products arrive from suppliers and are inspected, moved to inventory or production, final tested, packaged, and shipped to suppliers. There may be more than one hundred steps in the process. The potential for products to become lost, mixed, segregated, or mislabeled is high.

MATERIAL TRACKING TECHNIQUES

The following are well-established methods for tracking or tracing materials:

1. *Lot integrity control.* Batches or products are maintained intact. If rework is necessary, the affected products can be identified because all those from a uniform batch are positively tagged; if products are from a sub-batch, they can be traced to the parent batch.

2. *Processing control.* Each product or batch of products is uniquely identifiable. As the batch of products progresses through the production line, then work performed on the products is shown on processing documentation.

3. *Build control.* Components, subassembly, and assembly information is supplied with documentation indicating how material is assembled.

4. *Inspection and test.* Inspection and test results are shown on the documentation that follows material through the production process.

5. *Field activity and modification control.* Installation, maintenance, operation, or erection changes are also recorded and are traceable to the original design and production documents.[1]

HOW DO IDENTIFICATION AND TRACEABILITY CONTROL WORK?

Products can be controlled through the following identification methods:

- Control system is established and maintained for identifying products.

- Control system identifies authorities, responsibilities, procedures, documentation, marking, and dates.

- Each product or batch is uniquely coded and identified.

- Records and documents are maintained and accessible.

Products are also controlled through the following traceability methods:

- Control system is established and maintained for tracing products.

- Each product or batch is traceable through the production cycle into the customer's hands.

- Each product or batch is traceable to engineering prints, specifications, or other manufacturing data.

- Control system is forward-traceable from raw material to finished product.

THE EXPERT'S CORNER
Insights and Tips

We relied on each department to beef up and use their paper or electronics systems to assure product identification and traceability. Remember, you define what is meaningful/valuable for traceability in the event of a quality or waste situation. Whatever you develop should make good business sense and be easily understood on the shop floor.
BETH KRENZER,
Manager, Black and White Film
Manufacturing, Eastman Kodak

Data General labels all products manufactured with a part number, date code, and a unique serial number identifier. Data bases capture assembly/repair/test activities for each serial number. This process allows for forward and backward traceability. In the event of a quality problem, information such as how many products were built, shipped, and where the item resides can be determined by accessing the data bases. In addition to product identification, service contracts are also given unique identifiers. All service activities performed on a customer's system are recorded, including the names or badge numbers of the individuals who assisted with the call.

Software is identified through the design and development process by the use of tools. These tools allow control over who can make changes to the sources throughout the process. They also provide for the identification of each change of the software. In addition, identifiers are in the software when it is delivered to customers. This allows support functions to determine what software a customer is running.
JOANNE MAYO,
Corporate ISO Coordinator,
Data General

(continued)

This system, when applicable, can reduce costs in the event of a problem and also aids in the efficiency of the internal process control system.

DARYL PARKER,
Director, A.G.A. Quality,
ISO Registrar

Product traceability refers to tracing the product back to its origin. As an example, the manufacture of steel pipe is always performed with traceability from the tube back to the heat of steel from which it was cast. Traceability requirements should be carefully defined regarding the start and the end of the traceability. If applicable, separate identifiers should be used for personnel changes, changes in tooling, etc., and these identifiers should appear on the applicable inspection and stock records.

ANDREW BERGMAN,
Manager of Certification,
OTS Quality Registrars

4.9

Process Control

Factory work must be adapted to people, not people to machines.
PEHR GYLLENHAMMAR,
Managing Director, Volvo

QUICK SCAN
ISO 9001 Requirements

Production and major processes are controlled to prevent noncon-formances. Critical product characteristics are identified. Critical processes are in control and are capable of meeting specifications. Work instructions are developed for each job so employees under-stand responsibilities.

Special processes, those in which quality product characteristics cannot be fully verified, are also monitored and controlled.

WHAT IS GOOD MANUFACTURING?

Good manufacturing, like good engineering, follows some simple guidelines:

- Use the fewest number of parts.

- Simplify material movement.

- Eliminate buffer inventories.

- Use defect-free parts.

- Use modularity concepts.

- Minimize subassemblies.

- Apply new technology only when cost effective.

- Emphasize standardization, particularly with parts and materials.

- Use simplest assembly and fabrication operations.

- Know capability of machinery to meet specifications.

- Document information for each operation.

- Minimize machine setup time.

WHAT IS PROCESS CONTROL?

The purpose of process control is to confirm that operational and quality systems are producing uniform and consistent products or services. Production process control has different meanings. In the chemical process industry, for example, process control often involves computerized pressure-, volume-, and temperature-variable sensors and closed-feedback loops. In manufacturing, process control involves manual or computerized statistical measurement of critical product characteristics.

While the means of process control in the above two instances varies, the purpose and principle is the same. If a process changes, the operator or process engineer can identify the cause of the variation and determine the necessary correction. This requires that the process engineer or operator fully understand the process.

General Processes

Two types of processes are usually checked: general and specific. Process control involves identifying critical product characteristics and recognizing what process variables ensure the consistency of these product characteristics. Production process variables control critical product characteristics. These process variables may include one or more of the following:

- *Operator.* A new or inexperienced operator may overadjust a process. Proper selection and training of operators ensures that they are able to perform specified tasks correctly.

- *Materials.* Raw material varies in chemical or physical properties. Different suppliers may provide the same materials with different properties. Product testing, inspection, and certification of suppliers assures consistency.

- *Methods.* Procedures are different across shifts, plants, or operators. Checking work instructions minimizes the possibility of people doing the same thing differently.

- *Machines.* New fixture or tooling settings change. The process of approving new equipment or approving modified equipment ensures that the equipment is capable of meeting specifications.

- *Environment.* Humidity, heat, or contaminants change operational settings.

Special Processes

Some special processes shouldn't or can't be evaluated by the subsequent testing of its products. Sometimes deficient products are only discovered when they are in the customer's hands. This occurs in highly detailed or precise processes. In chemical processes, many variables interact to produce the product, and sometimes the interaction is not fully understood or controlled. For example, a minor change in temperature or pressure can change the physical properties of the product. Validation and documentation of the process variables focus on ensuring that the process is controlled as much as possible.

Special production processes may include investment casting, aluminum welding, heat treatment, and plastic fabrication. Special testing or inspections may include hydrostatic testing, liquid dye penetrant, tensile testing, or ultrasonic testing.

THE EXPERT'S CORNER
Insights and Tips

Flowcharting is a terrific tool to use to lay out your key processes. You can use flowcharts to develop procedures (or as a procedure) to check for appropriate controls to assure compliance to specifications. You never know. . . . ISO 9002 activities may even help you reengineer your operations and staffs for added productivity and quality.

We also did a lot of work on assuring that anyone making a quality decision had controlled and up-to-date standards.

BETH KRENZER,
Manager, Black and White Film
Manufacturing, Eastman Kodak

Manufacturing and servicing instructions are well documented. Work instructions are available for the assembly, test, and repair of each product and process (ie. machine, tools, test equipment). In addition, acceptable workmanship criteria have been established which meet national standards. Processes are developed by engineering and are assessed prior to release to standard production. Actual process performance is continually monitored and compared to process capability studies. Those processes determined to be out of control are flagged and corrected immediately by production personnel. Daily, weekly, and monthly quality results are monitored as well.

Software process controls are a combination of ISO compliant procedures, automated tools, coding standards, and good software engineering practices.

> JOANNE MAYO,
> Corporate ISO Coordinator,
> Data General

Controlling the processes that affect the quality of the product actually threads through business operations. Control fosters interaction with other parts of the organization, thus helping to reduce costs and provide more opportunities for improvement.

> DARYL PARKER,
> Director, A.G.A. Quality,
> ISO Registrar

The methods used to comply with this element depends upon the complexity of production, the type of attributes of measured characteristics, the prior knowledge of the process, and statistical control exhibited by the process.

The company should clearly identify the characteristics to control. Control of these characteristics is preferable to inspections.

> ANDREW BERGMAN,
> Manager of Certification,
> OTS Quality Registrars

4.10

Inspection and Testing

In testing, simulate the toughest condition your product is likely to encounter.

MARISA MANLEY, lawyer

QUICK SCAN
ISO 9001 Requirements

Inspection and testing can occur at each of the following production stages: incoming, in process, or final process.

A quality plan or similar procedure spells out how products are quality checked. Responsibilities and authorities for inspection, measurement, and testing are detailed in procedures.

Materials and products from suppliers are inspected and tested to determine compliance to requirements. Product inspection is one method of determining conformance.

In-process testing may involve product inspection and process control.

Final inspection and testing examines the entire product or system against requirements.

Inspection and test records are complete, current, and available.

IMPORTANCE OF INSPECTION AND TESTING

Quality responsibility has shifted from the buyer to the supplier. Customers require defect-free products delivered just-in-time, every time. The customer often does not rely on incoming inspection for verifying product quality because it is difficult to correct process errors merely by inspecting a shipment of products after the fact. To prevent or correct any problems, responsibility is moving upstream. The assumption is that if quality system controls are in place and operating properly, then products coming out of a process are consistent and satisfy requirements. This assumption applies to all operations, processes, and services. If the customer wants additional assurance, then receiving inspection can be conducted, which will only complement the supplier's own internal quality verification procedures.

However, production testing and inspection may never totally disappear. Regulatory authorities may still require that representative products be periodically tested. Customers may require suppliers to maintain clean rooms, laboratories, or separate testing facilities to provide consistent verification, calibration, and testing of machine parts, inspection equipment, fixtures, and gaging systems.

COMPUTERIZED INSPECTION AND TESTING

Automatic inspection equipment is capable of measuring 100 percent of a product's critical characteristics. Advances in microelectronics and process controls allow for the constant monitoring of a production operation and, if required, the inspection of each part. While these systems are expensive, they assure quick and accurate testing. The test equipment allows high measuring and evaluation rates, no contact between the measurement equipment and the part, and the ability to automatically link the data to a host computer for real-time analysis.[1]

Automated production inspection can also be used to monitor products at each process step. If there are unexpected variations within the specification limits, the equipment, through on-line process control, adjusts the process back to the target. Automated production inspection is especially useful for high-volume manufacturing where it is impossible to stop the production line to inspect parts. It is also helpful in flexible production operations where multiple products are produced.[2]

HOW INSPECTION AND TESTING CONTROL WORK

Products are controlled throughout the production process from incoming through final inspection. First, two key concepts, inspection and sampling, should be introduced. Inspection is the actual checking or verifying of product quality attributes for conformance to specifications. Sampling is the probability-based technique that determines the number of products to be pulled from a lot or batch for inspection. While inspection is usually not recommended because it is expensive and deficient products may still pass through and be approved, it is still performed for costly, life-extending, and one-of-a-kind products.

A principle of good production management is that critical quality areas, product characteristics, and process variables are identified, controlled, and documented. Products shouldn't be allowed to proceed down the production stream unless there is proof that quality has been verified and documented at critical quality points.

Receiving Inspection and Testing

Receiving or incoming inspection is the visual or dimensional check of product quality attributes. There are different methods of verifying purchased material quality. The choice of method depends on the type of purchased materials, past performance of the supplier, costs of inspection, and other variables.

Accurate inspection and testing require employees to have the ability to identify critical product characteristics, read engineering prints, and use critical measurement equipment. Testing processes are highly proceduralized and documented.

Incoming verification procedures also consider the supplier's process control and capability. The goal is to minimize incoming inspection and move toward prevention, using third-party certification, process controls, and other information.

In-Process Inspection and Testing

In-process testing involves the quality verification of products during production. Work instructions define who does what and when. As much as possible, targets and acceptable ranges define each critical process and/or product variable. Critical product characteristics are identified. Process variables responsible for producing these quality characteristics are controlled. Materials are tested at critical points of the production line because it is either too expensive or impossible to measure critical characteristics later in the production process. Measurement confirms that product characteristics are on target and within the required specification limits. Measurement equipment is controlled through calibration. If there is an instrument failure, a production person understands how to correct the problem.

Final Inspection and Testing

The purpose of final inspection is to verify that finished products satisfy requirements. Final inspection is a test or examination of the final system or entire product, not of component parts. In most cases it's already assumed that components satisfy requirements.

Inspection and Test Records

Inspection and test records show that incoming, in-process, or final tests have been completed and are satisfactory. Examples of controlled inspection and testing records consist of:

- Sampling and inspection plans.

- Capability studies.

- Statistical studies.

- Evidence of process control.

- Process control plans.

- First-item verification.

- In-process inspection and testing instructions.

THE EXPERT'S CORNER
Insights and Tips

You don't have to do it all yourself. We are continuing to make vendors and subcontractors responsible for the quality of the goods and services they provide. We continue to develop procedures and to decide on rules that they must follow.

In-process inspection and testing are performed throughout the manufacturing process to verify conformance to internal requirements. Final inspection and test are performed on manufacturing products to verify compliance with the final product requirements.

BETH KRENZER,
Manager, Black and White Film
Manufacturing, Eastman Kodak

Inspection and test stations are set up at key intervals within the manufacturing process, including receiving, in-process, and final assembly. Automated assembly equipment have the capability to test components prior to installation. Automated visual inspection and test equipment is utilized. Automated test processes can verify the proper configuration of a customer order and can ensure that the product operates as designed. In addition to the standard functional testing,

(continued)

extended testing and elevated temperature testing are often required as part of the test process. Extended reliability testing, such as Design Verification Test (DVT), Design Maturity Test (DMT), Reliability Verification Test (RVT), and Product Reliability Demonstration Test (PRDT) are performed on a sample of the product population.

Software inspection and testing are integral to the design, development, and release processes. Inspections occur during code and design reviews. Testing is done at the component level as well as the integration and system level. In addition, constant internal use of our software under development provides another form of feedback on the product's quality.

Other forms of testing also occur when we participate in the qualification of a third-party software product on a new release of the operating system. This supports our commitment to having full solutions available to our customers when a revision of the operating system is released.

JOANNE MAYO,
Corporate ISO Coordinator,
Data General

Product appraisal is interwoven with process control and should not be a separate entity. Strategically implemented, product testing plays an important role in validating performance and identifying areas for improvement.

DARYL PARKER,
Director, A.G.A. Quality,
ISO Registrar

Products shall not be dispatched until all appraisal activities have been completed and associated data approved. You can ship products if you have statistical confirmation that results will be good and if the customer is aware that material has not yet passed the certification. Dispatch is defined in this context as changing ownership.

ANDREW BERGMAN,
Manager of Certification,
OTS Quality Registrars

4.11

Inspection, Measuring, and Test Equipment

Efficiency and economy imply employment of the right instrument and material as well as their right use in the right manner.
LOUIS BRANDEIS,
Supreme Court Justice

QUICK SCAN
ISO 9001 Requirements

Inspection, measuring, and test equipment is properly identified, calibrated, and secured. Equipment tests are proceduralized and conducted under controlled conditions.

Measuring equipment is suitable for the accuracy and precision of the required tests.

Measuring equipment is identified and calibrated at set intervals against national or international standards.

Measuring equipment is positively identified.

Measuring equipment is calibrated and the calibration is thoroughly documented.

Measuring equipment, environmental conditions, records, software, and hardware are all controlled to ensure accuracy and precision.

QUALITY IS ONLY AS GOOD AS MEASURING AND TEST EQUIPMENT

Accurate data and information are essential for good decision making. Whether simple or high-tech, the equipment provides valuable information for making reliable decisions. The piece of equipment may be a micrometer or an automated, in-line gauge measuring five product quality characteristics, but either way, it must provide accurate and precise measurements.

The terms "accuracy" and "precision" have technical definitions. Accuracy is when a quality measurement consistently agrees with a standard or when measurements are located near the standard's target. Instrument calibration ensures accuracy. Precision

Ethyl's Experience

In the chemical industry, Ethyl Corporation has been a proactive ISO implementor. Ethyl wants to register all of its manufacturing units worldwide. Its Magnolia, Arkansas, plant, a producer of bromine and agricultural intermediates, became ISO 9002 registered and quickly saw the benefits of operational consistency.

The Magnolia plant is highly automated. Quality and safety depend on the accuracy of its monitoring and measuring equipment. Before the plant went through the registration process, pressure-control and other instruments were checked randomly, sometimes only after someone noticed a malfunction. Since the plant was registered, instruments are checked on a routine basis, thereby providing more consistent operations and offering a safer working environment for all employees.[1]

is when a series of measurements succeeds in obtaining the same value each time.

Operational decisions are based on good quality information and are assumed to be accurate, but at times this may not be the case because measuring and test equipment may have been misused, abused, or uncalibrated.

HOW ARE INSPECTION, MEASURING, AND TEST EQUIPMENT CONTROLLED?

To be accurate and precise, critical measurement systems must be used throughout the product development cycle. Control is maintained through the measurement system, which ensures that the proper measuring equipment is chosen and methods are developed so measurements are accurate and precise.

The objective of the inspection, measuring, and test equipment system is to secure useful information and data for intelligent decision making. How is this done?

- Standard measurement units are used.

- Customer, regulatory, or other calibration requirements are defined.

- The operator checks calibration of a piece of equipment prior to use and while using the instruments.

- Instruments of required accuracy and precision are selected to measure a quality attribute.

- All critical measurement equipment are identified.

- Methods of use, storage, and handling of the equipment are defined.

- Personnel are trained in the proper use, storage, and handling of the equipment.

- Calibration status of the equipment is indicated.

- Instruments are recalibrated following overuse, abuse, and misuse.

- If the gauge or instrument is used frequently, an operator checks it frequently to determine its precision and accuracy.

- Instruments are tagged with the date of calibration, name of calibrator, and date for recalibration.

- Instruments are recalibrated periodically.

- Equipment is calibrated against national or other standards.

- Calibration history is maintained.

CALIBRATION—THE KEY TO GOOD MEASUREMENT

Gauge repeatability and reproducibility (known as R&R studies) verify the accuracy and consistency of measurement instruments. Inspection tools—gauges—are accurate and precise in order to obtain repeatable measurements. Calibration is documented, maintained, and controlled. Procedures list the type of measurement equipment, along with its identification number, location, frequency of calibration, type of calibration, acceptance criteria, authorization for use, and corrective action, if equipment is nonconforming.

Sometimes the customer may specify the precision and accuracy of measuring instruments. These requirements are compared against process capabilities or contract requirements. If the instruments cannot maintain the required capability, then new instruments are purchased or this provision of the contract may have to be relaxed.

Inspection, measuring, and test equipment critical to product or process quality are identified, often tagged as a positive form of identification. At a minimum, the tag identifies the calibration status, the person performing the calibration, and the date when calibration will again be necessary. Other means of positive identification may also be used, such as computerized records. The point is that the user must be able to demonstrate that the equipment remains calibrated.

If a measurement or test system is out of calibration, previous measurements are checked for accuracy and precision. Products produced when critical measurement instruments were inaccurate may have to be retested. Records are updated to reflect the inaccurate measurements.

Furthermore, all test and measuring instruments are protected from misuse, abuse, or other hazards, which can cause misalignment or damage the equipment.

Sometimes test hardware, such as jigs and fixtures, are used in inspection. If these are misaligned, then the accuracy and precision can be affected. These should also be checked to prove that they are capable of maintaining test accuracy.

THE EXPERT'S CORNER
Insights and Tips

Like most companies, we used test equipment to ensure that our products were within specifications. We were also like many companies assuming that as long as the equipment worked, we did not have to worry about whether it was within calibration limits. We discovered the value of instrument calibration when we did the initial calibration. Most of our equipment was initially out of calibration, and when the newly calibrated equipment was put in place, we immediately noticed a 2 percent yield increase.

DAVID BALLARD,
quality consultant

We had to identify all measurement equipment used in our quality operation. Again we found flowcharting invaluable in identifying criti-

(continued)

cal inspection, testing, and measurement equipment. We then had to assure ourselves that the equipment was accurate and precise enough for our needs. In some cases, we actually reduced some testing and removed related equipment that wasn't needed.

BETH KRENZER,
Manager, Black and White Film
Manufacturing, Eastman Kodak

During the development of each division's ISO program, an evaluation of equipment on hand and anticipated usage was the first step to ensuring controls for calibration equipment. Some divisions already had a calibration system in place. Our challenge was how to deal with excess equipment as a result of downsizing operations and plant closures. Once usage was determined, excess equipment was gathered in a central location and sold. Excess equipment was inventoried and identified in a central database for each division, thereby allowing for easy recall.

JOANNE MAYO,
Corporate ISO Coordinator,
Data General

Inspection and test equipment must be controlled throughout an organization. Proper instrument control allows for accuracy in the process control system as well as other appraisal systems. It also can help reduce processing costs and identify areas for change.

DARYL PARKER,
Director, A.G.A. Quality,
ISO Registrar

A company shall have a calibration program verifying that equipment is capable of the necessary accuracy and precision. This means gauges are calibrated properly and calibration records are maintained so all personnel know the status of the instruments. It also helps to think of measuring as a process made up of raw materials, equipment, and procedures.

ANDREW BERGMAN,
Manager of Certification,
OTS Quality Registrars

4.12

Inspection and Test Status

If you can't measure it, you can't manage it.
ANONYMOUS

QUICK SCAN
ISO 9001 Requirements

Inspection and test status of products is identified throughout production. Status can be indicated by marking or tagging. Status may indicate product inspection, testing, or disposition status.

CAN THIS MATERIAL BE USED?

Production materials can go through a hundred or more process steps. How do plant and production people know the status of the material? Has the material been tested? Is it okay to use? There has to be some method to clearly identify the status of materials as they go through the production process from incoming through partial assembly, final assembly, final inspection, and installation.

The status of the material indicates:

1. Does the material need to be tested?

2. Has it been tested yet?

3. Has it been tested and approved?

4. Has it been tested and rejected?

As usual, this quality system works on the principle of exception. Conforming materials go through production or into inventory. Nonconforming materials or products are red tagged or appropriately labeled, then segregated so corrective action can be initiated.

Inspection, measuring, and test equipment are used in incoming, in-process, and final inspection and testing. Measurement equipment is also used and controlled throughout the design, manufacture, and installation of products. Test status may be indicated in various ways, including:

- Labels.

- Inspection records.

- Authorization stamps.

- Test analyses and records.

- Physical stamps.

- Test software.

- Authorization stamps.

- Inspection and test status stamps.

- Material disposition tags.

THE EXPERT'S CORNER
Insights and Tips

The labels, routing, cards, hold tags, and computer holds had to be reviewed for effectiveness and defined in procedures. This is a great clause to get operational groups to mistake-proof/fail-safe their test and measurement systems.

> BETH KRENZER,
> Manager, Black and White Film
> Manufacturing, Eastman Kodak

A process flow, including each inspection and test station, is defined for every product type. Upon the completion of inspection or test the employee records acceptance or rejection information by logs/tags or on-line. Production, test, and inspection status can be accessed by referencing a serial number, a work order number, or a sales order number in the electronic data base. Rejected products require repair, reinspection and/or retest prior to moving to the next operation.

Software test status is monitored throughout the development process. Test reports are required input to the process for making a release decision.

> JOANNE MAYO,
> ISO Corporate Coordinator,
> Data General

Test status should be maintained throughout production to designate that products have passed through the required controls and that they have passed/failed inspection. Records should identify the responsible authority for the release of conforming products and all required controls have been completed. Status may be indicated by marking, tagging, or signing off—either physically or electronically. While physical segregation may be the only effective means, in an automated environment, accurate disposition may be accomplished through the database.

> ANDREW BERGMAN,
> Manager of Certification,
> OTS Quality Registrars

4.13

Control of Nonconforming Product

In complex systems, malfunction and even total nonfunction may not be detectable for long periods, if ever.

MELVIN SYKES, lawyer

QUICK SCAN
ISO 9001 Requirements

Nonconforming products are identified, assessed, segregated, and disposed of according to approved procedures.

Nonconforming products may be scrapped, reworked, used as is, or returned to the supplier.

HOW ARE NONCONFORMING PRODUCTS CONTROLLED?

One of the worst nightmares for a customer *and* a supplier is the shipment of nonconforming products. The customer may have to recall products or sustain the cost of a field repair, which is very expensive. The supplier may lose the customer's business. How can this be prevented? Proper identification and segregation of nonconforming products can prevent this problem. Immediate corrective action should fix and eliminate the symptom and the root cause of the problem.

One method of controlling products is through bar-coding. The major advantage of bar-coding over manually keying the information into a computer is that there is less chance of error and it is faster. It is a positive method of identifying conforming and nonconforming materials.

Bar-coding is already extensively used in the retail business. Most retail products have a universal product bar code identifying the product. When a customer purchases the product, the checker waves a wand over it and its cost is automatically calculated. The information is sent to a computer that maintains inventory, count, cost, and other information. A store's management can use this information to order new products and to obtain buying information. The bar code conforms to a well-defined set of rules.[1]

Control of Nonconforming Products

How can a company assure that no nonconforming products are sent to the customer? Once a process deficiency is discovered, nonconforming products must be segregated from conforming products. Nonconforming products should be identified, segregated, and disposed of in such a manner that they can't be improperly used. Personnel are trained to prevent the inadvertent delivery or use of nonconforming products by the customer. Throughout the process, proper records are maintained. The important point is the system should be foolproof.

If nonconforming products should be delivered, then the customer is immediately informed. Corrective action is implemented to ensure that it doesn't recur and correction is pushed upstream into production or engineering. Design reviews or process controls are initiated to prevent the recurrence.

Nonconformity Review and Disposition

Nonconformances are such an important deviation or exception from an operating quality system that the reasons for nonconformances must be fully understood. Personnel are selected for reviewing the cause of the nonconformity and personnel are authorized to dispose of the nonconforming products. Personnel determining disposition are aware of the approved disposition options. Once the decision is made, then records reflect the decisions made.

Nonconforming products may then be:

- Reworked.

- Accepted as is.

- Regraded.

- Scrapped.

THE EXPERT'S CORNER
Insights and Tips

We had to ensure that all nonconforming products were clearly identified either physically or on computer records, in order to segregate them from conforming products. We had to clearly define who had responsibility and what guidelines were used if the products had to be regraded for another application.

ISO is a real world. Say what you do and do what you say. We found we had to tighten up on some documentation practices and in particular we had to document the decision-making process our professional people were using.

BETH KRENZER,
Manager, Black and White Film
Manufacturing, Eastman Kodak

(continued)

Product or material deemed to be nonconforming to Data General's specifications are marked in some fashion, usually by affixing a discrepancy tag, and moved to a separate area for disposition. Products that require the review of engineering are held until a determination of action can be made. Products that can be repaired in-house are moved to the appropriate areas and must be reinspected and retested prior to being returned as part of available inventory. Scrapped products and materials are segregated for recycling or disposal. Any items which are determined to be inappropriate for customer shipments but are still useable in-house are identified in a permanent manner to prevent accidental use in a customer order.

In compliance with ISO 9001 requirements, decisions to release a software product always include the consideration of open problem reports related to the revision under development. We balance the need to ensure that a revision is stable against the desire to fix every problem that has been identified. A rigorous process is applied to determining which problems are fixed and which are deferred.

Once a software product is released, we continue to accept problem reports from both customers and internal users. These problem reports are investigated and resolved, both for current customers and in the subsequent development projects underway.

JOANNE MAYO,
ISO Corporate Coordinator,
Data General

Evaluation of the cause of nonconforming products provides a basis for identifying opportunities for improvement. It also is an indicator of process efficiency and provides valuable information to management.
DARYL PARKER, Director,
A.G.A. Quality, ISO Registrar

The control system for nonconforming product usually includes clear identification of the deficiencies, location of the deficient products, and description of the nonconformity. A reporting system must be in place to confirm that all employees who perform work that affects quality are kept informed.

Personnel with the authority to dispose of nonconforming product shall not feel pressured to release material because of schedule concerns before the procedure is followed. Likewise, a climate should not exist that "punishes" employees for discovering or disposing of nonconforming products.

ANDREW BERGMAN,
Manager of Certification,
OTS Quality Registrars

4.14

Corrective Action

Often, the most significant feature of good . . . work is that it has kept something bad from happening to the company. How can we measure bad things that do not happen?

ROBERT TOMASKO,
management consultant

QUICK SCAN
ISO 9001 Requirements

Corrective action is fixing and eliminating the symptom and root cause of deficiencies and/or nonconformances. The first challenge is to determine why the deficiency occurred by examining data. A plan detailing how the corrective action will be carried out is then developed. If the problem is chronic or systemic, then a monitoring mechanism is established to ensure that it doesn't recur.

WHAT IS CORRECTIVE ACTION?

The concept of corrective action originated in regulated industries where critical deficiencies are life threatening. Regulatory agencies requiring corrective action systems include the Food and Drug Administration (for pharmaceutical products), the Federal Communications Commission (for telecommunications

159

products), and the Environmental Protection Agency (for environmental conservation and product disposal). These agencies audit companies in their sectors and issue a corrective action request to correct any noncompliance of a statutory provision.

Parts-per-Million Production Quality

Nippondenso Manufacturing USA was recently honored by *Industry Week* magazine for having one of America's best plants. Quality runs at a 1.2-parts-per-million defect level. One of the main reasons for this high quality level is Nippondenso's corrective action system. The system discovers problems and corrects them so they don't recur.

Defects discovered by the customer are assessed by an interdisciplinary technical team. The team attacks problems at their root cause, determining and assigning counter and preventive measures to confirm that there is a permanent fix. An independent quality-assurance group subsequently audits the process to ensure that solutions work and systems catch problems before the customer.[1]

HOW CORRECTIVE ACTION ELIMINATES RECURRENT DEFICIENCIES

An operational problem or deficiency may be detected through an audit, through operational monitoring, field failure, out-of-control conditions, or customer complaint. The problem may be critical, major, minor, recurring, systemic, or chronic. The important thing is to intervene before the problem becomes critical and is life threatening.

Once problems or deficiencies are encountered, there has to be a system for eliminating the symptom and the root cause. Procedures define who does what, when, and how to resolve the nonconformance and to determine the effectiveness of the corrective action.

The effectiveness of corrective action may be monitored through quality systems, customer complaints, or field failures. Regardless of the cause, each is a red flag of a system deterioration. The assumption is that if the quality processes and systems are in place and operating properly, then there shouldn't be any deficiencies.

If a deficiency should occur, the customer is immediately informed. A formal plan is then devised to decide what will be done so the problem doesn't recur.

In some cases, major changes, such as a design, packaging, or manufacturing change, may have to be instituted. The level of prevention reflects the level of nonconformance. Responsibility and authority are defined so problems don't recur. Chronic or systemic problems require an interdisciplinary solution to coordinate, document, and monitor the corrective action. Often corrective action is the responsibility of the area where the problem occurred.

Corrective action may well change the basic quality system. If operations, processes, or systems are changed as a result of the corrective action, then procedures are rewritten to conform to the new processes.

PROBLEMS AND CRISES INITIATE AUDITS

Auditing and corrective action go hand in hand. ISO or internal audits assess the state of internal or external quality systems. If the systems don't exist, are not working properly, are not documented, or are not understood by personnel, then a corrective action request is issued.

Two types of audits are routinely conducted—compliance and improvement. In compliance auditing, such as ISO 9000, the objective is to determine compliance or noncompliance with specific provisions of the ISO standard. In improvement auditing, the focus is on eliminating error and waste, improving processes and systems, benchmarking internal performance, measuring performance, or pleasing customers.

Corrective action is often initiated in response to a problem or crisis, which may be a customer complaint or product recall. Continuing customer satisfaction was the impetus for Raytek, a manufacturer of temperature measurement instruments, to develop a corrective action effort. In 1986, customers were complaining about quality and returned products to Raytek because of product performance, as well as delivery and shipping problems. The company was also failing to track customer complaints and follow up to be sure that customers were satisfied. The company heard the message. To track quality performance, Manufacturing, Engineering, and others got together to review each returned product within the one-year warranty period. The goal was to discover the cause of the problem and authorize people to solve it to the customer's satisfaction. Chronic problems required intensive analysis to eliminate the root cause.[2]

DETERMINING THE CAUSE

The cause of infrequent or random events is difficult to determine. These events may be part of the background noise of any operation or system. If they are inconsequential, they may be tolerated as part of the system, but if they can cause major problems, their cause needs to be determined, and doing so can be time consuming and very difficult.

The goal of failure analysis is to understand how and why a failure occurred. The analysis leads to corrective action and other preventive measures. The objective in failure analysis is to understand the true cause of the problem so it doesn't recur.

One method for preventing failure is to establish realistic system procedures and to follow them consistently. Procedures aren't written in stone. If there is a better way to do something, the method is analyzed and, if necessary, incorporated into an up-dated procedure.[3]

In determining causes of process or system failure, common patterns seem to consistently arise, specifically:

- High variation in purchased materials.

- Variation in production processes, tooling, equipment, or dies.

- Improper storage, handling, or movement of products.

- Poor training or supervision of personnel.

- Inadequate or poor operating methods and/or instructions.

- Poor environmental or working conditions.

The Five Most Common Deficiencies

David Ballard, an ISO consultant, was involved in one of the first ISO registrations in the United States. He discovered that deficiencies requiring correction fall within five categories: documents, equipment, material, personnel, and corrective action. Specifically, they are:

DOCUMENTS

Unapproved documents.
Procedures do not correspond to practice.
Unauthorized changes.
Superseded documents in use.
Documents not located according to distribution.
Approved supplier list not complete.
Product releases do not include review of records.
Record-keeping deficiencies.

EQUIPMENT

New equipment not qualified.
Calibration incomplctc.
Handling arrangements inadequate.
Product packaging does not protect quality.
Inadequate reaction to process out of control additions.

MATERIAL

Inadequate or no identification.
Material obtained from unapproved source.
Material in poor condition.
Inadequate shelf-life control.
Inspection status not clear.
Nonconforming material not isolated.

PERSONNEL

Not trained or qualified for task.
Not aware of requirements.
Not complying with documented requirements.
Responsibilities not defined.

CORRECTIVE ACTION

Use as is—used excessively.
Nonconformances not identified.
Corrective action not determined.
Corrective action slow or not implemented.

ELIMINATING THE SYMPTOM AND
THE ROOT CAUSE

Fixing the symptom means identifying the problem, understanding it, and fixing its outward manifestations. The symptom may or may not involve the root cause. If the problem recurs, then the symptom has only been fixed and not the root cause.

The root cause of the problem may not be easy to detect. It may require complex testing and analysis of different systems, processes, or product variables. Often, this requires specialists to uncover the process variables and eliminate those that cause the problem. Eliminating the fix and the root cause creates more uniform operations, which are the essence of a quality operation.

CLOSING THE LOOP

Closed-loop corrective action is a continuous-improvement tool for coordinating information within and across the organization so problems can be solved as they arise. The closed loop ensures that the problems don't recur, and that operations are monitored and controlled.

Who is responsible for ensuring the success of closing the loop in corrective action? As departmental boundaries dissolve through organizational reengineering, multidisciplinary teams are being given the responsibility for maintaining, monitoring, and improving operations. And as problems occur, a multidisciplinary team or work area team is responsible for eliminating the root case and ensuring they do not recur.[4]

ANTICIPATING PROBLEMS

It is no longer sufficient just to correct problems as they occur. Areas of risk must be anticipated and systems need to be established to monitor and, it is hoped, preempt a problem from occurring. This type of feed-forward corrective action requires organizational personnel to understand the strengths and weaknesses of its internal systems. If the risks are high, more internal controls are developed. For example, in areas where the cost of failure is high or an injury can result, more controls are implemented. Internal controls may consist of training personnel, monitoring equipment, auditing periodically, or stepping up on documenting processes.

THE EXPERT'S CORNER
Insights and Tips

One of the important things we learned in software development is to close the corrective action loop: plan . . . do . . . test . . . fix . . . retest . . . release. Thus, we make sure that what gets fixed really works and works correctly.

EMILY KONOLD,
QA Specialist, Help/Systems

Performing tasks per written ISO procedures has improved consistency in our building and testing products. And coupled with the additional training (over 60 hours per employee in the last nine months), closer relationship with subcontractors, and a working corrective action system, "fire drills" are now the exception rather than the norm.

JESS HAGEMEYER,
Director of Product Quality,
VMX Industries

A prevention attitude has been implemented throughout the organization, accompanied by an early-detection and corrective action system. This provides evidence not only of a quality management system but of positive quality attitudes and management commitment to continuous improvement. This has resulted in statistically significant improvements at Dow Corning's first-time approval rate, customer complaint frequency, and compliance to customer-required dates.

LES SCHNOLL,
ISO 9000 Manager, Dow Corning

We decided to trigger corrective action through audits of quality systems, customer complaints, nonconformances in manufacturing or testing, or any type of situation regarding production. Departments used different forms to capture and follow up closure of corrective action.

In hindsight it may have been wiser to require more standardization of our corrective action paperwork. Corrective action systems will often trigger a problem-solving team effort. For Black and White Film Manufacturing, our corrective action system has become one of the biggest benefits of our ISO 9002 efforts. Corrective action has allowed us to keep improving our quality system in a logical and systematic way.

BETH KRENZER,
Manager, Black and White Film
Manufacturing, Eastman Kodak

Within Data General's divisional quality systems there are many mechanisms to address corrective action, from vendor notification to the customer complaint resolution system. In addition to the standard processes already established (i.e., material purge system, product hold notification, hardware and software problem resolution, process and product change requests), we developed a process to handle corrective action resolution when all other systems were either not appropriate or were not effective. This corrective action process allows any employee to identify a problem and present it to appropriate management. Here again, the electronic office system is used to distribute, track, and retain corrective action notices. The system can be used between divisions as well (i.e., Manufacturing to Design or Service to Manufacturing). This system provides a mechanism so that even the most complex issues are identified, addressed, and resolved.

Problem tracking for software products and processes is provided through tools which are accessible to all members of the software development community. It is the responsibility of all employees to report problems as well as investigate and resolve problems which have been assigned to them. All problems are evaluated for root causes, and resolutions are put in place to prevent future occurrences.

JOANNE MAYO,
Corporate ISO Coordinator,
Data General

Corrective action quality systems provide the ultimate basis for continuous improvement in a company. An effective system analyzes all work

(continued)

processes in a company, leading to elimination of waste and reduction in costs. Valuable information is also provided to management regarding the performance of the company.

DARYL PARKER,
Director, A.G.A. Quality,
ISO Registrar

A company should distinguish between corrective action and preventive action. The company's corrective action procedure should identify who is responsible for originating a corrective action request and who it should be issued to. The assessment team should evaluate whether the auditee's CAR system is adequately structured; whether its CAR's are effective; whether the auditee modified its corrective action process since initial implementation; whether they, the auditors, have recognized any trends; whether the system is comprehensive enough for them to recognize trends, and whether they have modified any related procedures resulting from corrective action.

ANDREW BERGMAN,
Manager of Certification,
OTS Quality Registrars

4.15

Handling, Storage, Packaging, and Delivery

QUICK SCAN
ISO 9001 Requirements

Handling, storage, packaging, and delivery of products are planned, controlled, and documented.

Handling control considers the transportation of material to prevent damage, deterioration, or contamination due to vibration, corrosion, temperature, or deteriorating conditions.

Storage control considers the physical security, identification, and environmental factors affecting the composition of materials.

Packaging considers the procedures, materials, labeling, and other factors that protect products against deterioration or contamination during storage or transport.

Delivery control ensures the protection of products during shipping.

GROWING IMPORTANCE OF HANDLING, STORAGE, PACKAGING, AND DELIVERY

As more companies develop quality initiatives, success and failure in the marketplace will be in the details of execution, the total execution of the quality initiative and, most importantly, the customer's total experience with a company.

A product can be well designed and manufactured, but if the customer doesn't receive it in perfect condition, then he or she will be dissatisfied. Products can deteriorate, be damaged, or be contaminated during storage, handling, or delivery. Sturdy packaging, timely delivery, good handling, and safe storage are all critical to customer satisfaction as much as the product itself.

GE Supply, a division of General Electric Company, is pursuing the goal of error-free transactions. GE Supply's goal is to have a seamless, fluid product delivery system to satisfy individual market niches.[1] Its quality systems, such as procedures, materials, design, and labels, are all designed to provide sufficient protection for error-free delivery.[2]

Product storage, handling, and packaging are more important today than they used to be because the risks of failure—spills, litigation, and so forth—are much higher. Chemical trucks that overturn or railroad cars that derail with concentrated chemicals have much more potential to cause widespread damage and loss of life. The amount of medical wastes is also increasing, as is the cost of collection, handling, and disposition of such wastes.

HANDLING, STORAGE, PACKAGING, AND DELIVERY CONTROLS

Handling, storing, and transporting products are costly, prone to error, and have high accident rates because they are labor intensive. Throughout the process, personnel are used to receive, store, shelve, move, count, inspect, repair, retrofit, package, label, and assemble products.

Again, consistency is the key to preventing product damage, contamination, or deterioration in the handling, storage, packaging, and movement or transfer of materials. These should be seamless activities. To ensure consistency, product handling, storage, packaging, and labeling are controlled throughout product development and delivery.

Product Handling

Material handling may involve containers, conveyors, vehicles, tanks, pallets, or other conveyance systems. Procedures should detail how products are handled to prevent damage from abrasion, shock, or vibration. Products with distinctive properties are specially handled and protected. Liquids are not mixed and products are not exposed to destructive environments. Electronic components are handled and stored in antistatic containers.

Product Storage

Materials are stored so they don't deteriorate due to corrosion, temperature, or adverse environmental conditions. Storage areas are secured and protected from environmental degradation. Stored products are regularly checked to verify quality and, if required, to extend shelf life. Materials may also be quarantined, segregated, or held in bonded areas. Storage facilities and containers are selected with the product characteristics, humidity, contents, pressure rating, regulatory requirements, and safety requirements in mind.

Product Packaging

The basic purpose of packaging is to hold materials or products. But packaging also identifies contents, maintains cleanliness, eliminates moisture, advertises products, protects contents, and

Changing Storage Requirements

The storage of products has probably not changed much in 50 years. However, the pressures of maintaining safety, ensuring flexibility, preserving simplicity, maintaining space, and complying with labeling requirements have changed the methods for storing products. Storage requirements are considered early in product development and are designed so quality is maintained throughout the product lifecycle. Storage design may be determined by the ergonomics of the work space, worker capabilities, space utilization, pickup time, security accessibility, product protection, inventory control, and storage requirements.[3]

provides instructions for operation and maintenance. Contents, materials, loading, product characteristics, and customer requirements are important when choosing packaging. Packaging may have to be dedicated so as not to contaminate the next shipment.

Labeling

Labeling has also become much more important because of regulatory requirements. Traditionally, a label informed the buyer of a package's contents, or was decorative. Now labels have to conform to the size, content, and design requirements spelled out in national, state, and local regulations.[4]

Product Delivery

Product delivery is also changing, due to just-in-time requirements, transportation economics, and governmental regulations. Transportation services are trying to provide more value to the customer through, for example, simplified freight tariffs, just-in-time delivery, sequenced delivery, and special packaging.

Products can be stored in many types of containers, including bottles, jars, cans, bags, cartons, or cases. Safety and regulatory requirements are critical in storage and packaging. Ingested products are shipped in childproof and tamperproof containers. In many states, beverage containers are recycled.

THE EXPERT'S CORNER
Insights and Tips

We learned this labor-intensive process can be automated. For example, we put in a bar-coding system for shipping all of our products.
EMILY KONOLD,
Q.A. Specialist, Help/Systems

Again, we found it helpful to look at the flowchart of the manufacturing process and pinpoint areas where we needed procedures for adequate handling, storage, packaging, and delivery in order to minimize waste and assure our customers of high-quality products.
BETH KRENZER,
Manager, Black and White Film
Manufacturing, Eastman Kodak

This clause was not an issue for us. Data General designs unit packaging for each new product and special in-process product carriers which ensures that products are not damaged during handling and shipping. Automated material storage units are also utilized in many areas. Sophisticated inventory and work-in-process tracking systems are in place to confirm that customer orders are delivered on time. Mainly two areas had to be addressed in order to comply with the ISO standard: (1) control of time-sensitive material and (2) periodic assessment of inventory condition.

Extensive product release and verification procedures have been put in

(continued)

*place to ensure that the right software product, as agreed to during
the software release decision process, is released to manufacturing to be
shipped to Data General customers.*

*Within Systems Development, handling methods to prevent electrosta-
tic discharge (ESD) damage to engineering prototypes had to be introduced. Since the effects of mishandling were seldom identifiable, it
required extensive employee training and management reinforcement to
obtain compliance to the process requirements.*

> Joanne Mayo,
> Corporate ISO Coordinator,
> Data General

*Criteria shall be established with which to evaluate the condition of
materials in storage. Provisions for storage shall be addressed, including
identification, care, maintenance, and segregation.*

> Andrew Bergman,
> Manager of Certification,
> OTS Quality Registrars

4.16

Quality Records

Information may be accumulated in files, but it must be retrieved to be of use in decision making.

KENNETH ARROW, economist

Quick Scan
ISO 9001 Requirements

Quality records are generated and maintained throughout the organization for all critical activities to ensure that products meet requirements.

Quality records are properly prepared, stored, secured, maintained, and updated so they are identifiable, accurate, complete, and current.

GROWTH OF COMPLEX RECORDS AND DOCUMENTATION

As products and operations become more complex, the volume of product information and records correspondingly increases. For example, at Northern Telecom's Digital Switching Divisions plant, simple shop instructions were initially collated in a typed manual that was used as a reference and teaching document for new full-time operators. This document was the employee bible, as new operators were expected to build relatively simple telephones from memory. Operators are now expected to learn more than one operation, to work on multifunctional teams, to actively solve process problems, and to work on more complex systems. Workers are now cross trained. Work instructions are more complex, incorporating piece part pictures, placement instructions, inspection information, and critical product parameters.[1]

HOW ARE RECORDS CONTROLLED?

Quality systems are only as good as their records and documentation. Records prove that quality has been specified, controlled, verified, and improved. The entire quality management system relies on documentation detailing who does what and when. If actions are undertaken as a result of a quality discrepancy, quality records indicate what was affected and how it was resolved.

ISO quality auditors and line personnel use quality records to verify the effectiveness of quality systems. As the amount of information increases, quick access becomes more important. For that reason, records, which used to be in a paper format, are now often in an electronic medium for easy access and storage.

Documentation access, safety, retention time, storage, and backup are important issues to be addressed in procedures:

- *Access.* Who has access to confidential and/or proprietary information?

- *Safety.* Are records stored in a safe and secure area?

- *Retention time.* Do regulatory or customer requirements spell out retention times?

- *Storage.* Are documents stored in a secure environment to minimize deterioration, damage, or loss?

- *Backup.* If there is a catastrophe, are there duplicate records?

THE EXPERT'S CORNER
Insights and Tips

We stayed away from too many records. The less paperwork, the more effective we thought we were. We have gained a new appreciation for these records. We can provide auditors or customers with complete records on all products produced. When a complaint does come in, we are usually able to identify and investigate the problem within a few hours.

DAVID BALLARD,
quality consultant

We thought through the issues of retention time and appropriate storage responsibilities of our quality records. Analysis of these records enabled us to see trends that could be used in any recall situation. Another consideration was how we should comply with our customer's requirements.

BETH KRENZER,
Manager, Black and White Film
Manufacturing, Eastman Kodak

As a computer manufacturer, most of our quality records are maintained on-line (computerized). As in the case of our document control system, quality records are stored in public drawers so they can be accessed by any individual requiring the information. Quality records retained in specific software programs designed to collect or track product/service activities are stored in databases.

JOANNE MAYO,
Corporate ISO Coordinator,
Data General

(continued)

Historical records can be invaluable as a source of information for management. An efficient system of storage and retrieval of documents can dramatically prevent deficiencies and reduce costs.

> DARYL PARKER,
> Director, A.G.A. Quality,
> ISO Registrar

The company's process must include provision for the identification, collection, indexing, filing, storage, maintenance, and disposition of quality records. Pertinent supplier records must also be retained. Retention periods for records should be established and records should be retrievable and well maintained.

> ANDREW BERGMAN,
> Manager of Certification,
> OTS Quality Registrars

4.17

Internal Quality Audits

Feedback is the breakfast of champions.
KENNETH H. BLANCHARD, author

QUICK SCAN
ISO 9001 Requirements

Internal quality audits are conducted to verify whether quality system elements are effective and are suitable to achieving quality objectives.

Quality audits are planned, conducted, and reported according to authorized procedures.

Areas may be reaudited to evaluate efficiency, effectiveness, and economy of corrective actions.

WHAT IS A QUALITY AUDIT?

Two types of quality auditing are usually conducted. The first type is used to determine compliance to ISO standards criteria. This type of auditing is fairly static in terms of determining compliance or noncompliance with technical and quality standards, specifications, procedures, drawings, and other quality documentation. The second type of auditing goes beyond

179

examining compliance and looks for opportunities for improvement and productivity.

Both types of audits share common elements. In general, a quality audit is an objective and often independent assessment of an area or activity. A commonly accepted definition of quality auditing is: "a systematic examination of the acts and decisions by people with respect to quality, in order to independently verify or

Ten Objectives of Internal Quality Auditing

1. Increase internal and external customer satisfaction.

2. Obtain accurate, reliable, and relevant operating and quality information.

3. Appraise operations and quality systems in an objective and independent manner.

4. Identify and minimize risks.

5. Ensure that organizational objectives are achieved and improved.

6. Confirm that quality controls are in place and operating properly.

7. Comply with customer, quality, regulatory, and other requirements.

8. Plan, conduct, and report the audit professionally.

9. Report results that are understandable, doable, and relevant to the organization.

10. Focus on improving internal controls to prevent nonconformances and to improve operations.

evaluate and report compliance to the operational requirements of the quality program or the specification or contract requirement of the product or service."[1]

WHY CONDUCT QUALITY AUDITS?

Quality audits are the major assessment and assurance tool for evaluating internal operations and suppliers. In terms of internal operations, quality audits provide evidence that quality systems are continuing to be effective in satisfying quality requirements. In terms of suppliers, audits indicate not just whether the supplier is capable or is complying with customer requirements, but whether the supplier continues to improve.

Continuous improvement requires that systems and processes be periodically evaluated through audits to determine whether they are operating according to procedures as well as whether they are capable of being improved. In statistical jargon, this is called determining whether the system is in control and capable.

The authority for internal quality audits is stated in a management policy. The policy defines the scope, authority, responsibility, reporting procedures, and follow-up responsibilities of the auditor, auditee, and customer.

Audits involve three parties: auditor, auditee, and customer. Each party has specific responsibilities and accountabilities. The customer authorizes the audit and is often the recipient of the report. The auditor conducts the audit. The auditee is the party being audited.

Internal auditors accumulate information to arrive at an opinion. External ISO auditors evaluate quality systems to determine compliance with ISO criteria.

WHO CONDUCTS THE AUDITS?

Internal auditing is sometimes conducted by a quality auditor from a staff department such as Quality Auditing or from a line operations group. Typically, Quality Auditing is a separate group focusing on supplier, cost, and operational issues. Nowadays, as quality takes on a greater importance, Quality Auditing is being incorporated into operations. For example, Xerox Corporation has decided that its audit staff must use quality tools, speak a quality language, and participate in quality improvement teams. Motorola views its auditors not as TQM assessors but as auditors doing TQM. Solectron sees internal quality auditors as business partners, as internal advisers on how to improve business processes.[2]

THE THREE STAGES OF A QUALITY AUDIT

There are three stages in a quality audit:

- Planning.
- Conducting.
- Reporting.

The Nine Critical Steps in Quality Planning[3]

1. Understand customer requirements.
2. Notify the auditee.
3. Understand the auditee.
4. Develop preliminary audit survey.
5. Interview the auditee.
6. Develop audit objectives.
7. Identify and evaluate audit risk.
8. Evaluate internal controls.
9. Prepare the audit plan.

Planning the Quality Audit

Experienced quality auditors spend much time preparing for the quality audit. This includes understanding customer requirements, understanding the auditee's quality processes, and developing a plan to obtain the required information without disrupting the auditee's operations. Proper planning provides the necessary focus to confirm that the quality audit satisfies the audit objectives and pleases the ultimate customer. Planning minimizes the time spent chasing false leads, chasing insignificant items, reaching dead ends, and missing major deficiencies.

Conducting the Quality Audit

In implementing the ISO 9000 quality audit, the quality auditor will verify and evaluate compliance of quality systems, processes, and products against requirements. Requirements are specified in quality standards, engineering drawings, procedures, work instructions, and contracts.

The internal quality auditor may have a broader mandate than simply determining compliance or conformance to written requirements. The internal quality auditor may well look at productivity, safety, environmental factors, efficiency, profitability, improvement, disclosure, and other factors.

Reporting the Quality Audit Results

The quality audit should satisfy and provide value to the customer. The audit report may conclude that everything is satisfactory or that there are deficiencies. If there are deficiencies, the auditor will issue a corrective action request for critical and major deficiencies.

CLOSING THE LOOP

How does one know if the corrective action has been properly implemented? Well, if the same or similar deficiencies recur, then the original fix or correction was not implemented or not implemented properly.

Several things can be done to close the audit loop, including:

• Reaudit a specific process.

• Confirm corrective action.

• Confirm promises of corrective action.

• Monitor corrective action over time.

THE EXPERT'S CORNER
Insights and Tips

By conducting internal audits, we learned the importance and advantages of being able to find things out ourselves before the ISO auditors came back. This helped to get our operations corrected and working more effectively much earlier.

EMILY KONOLD,
Q.A. Specialist, Help/Systems

Quality auditing really helped our company for ISO 9000 registration, and we also used it as an employee involvement tool. Each audit area uses a different set of auditors from the manufacturing area. We currently use these audits to help identify problem areas not only in quality, but also in safety, production, and communications.

DAVID BALLARD,
quality consultant

In my experience, internal system auditing is undoubtedly the most powerful element of the ISO 9000 requirements. Internal auditing is the real-time, on-line method of prevention by auditing the system that creates your product or service. Effective internal system auditing provides problem prevention long before your customer or bottom line tells you about problems.

NORM SEIFERT,
quality consultant, TQMA

Whether you do the internal audit or hire an external party for your internal audits, you need to think through logistics, corrective action processes, and communications processes for internal audits.

Internal audits have been a terrific tool for us to improve our quality systems and to spread quality systems ideas across departments. For example, we have people from the cutting and boxing areas in Black and White Film Manufacturing audit the coating area and vice versa. Our internal audit procedures specify that one can't audit one's own department, but we take advantage of the fact that we have a large organization to help each other in internal auditing.

BETH KRENZER,
Manager, Black and White Film
Manufacturing, Eastman Kodak

Although Data General's quality system included appropriate process and product audits, there was no formal internal quality system audit program. This process had to be developed by each division in order to meet ISO requirements. We chose to send selected employees to external auditor training for two reasons: (1) Internal expertise was utilized to implement the ISO programs, thus eliminating the need for outside consultants and (2) employees in all divisions received a consistent message. Auditors are drawn from all ranks (operator to management), which provides a mix of perspectives. The majority of the auditors have over ten years' experience with the company, although this is not a requirement. Employees see experience with ISO as an enhancement to their career growth.

JOANNE MAYO,
Corporate ISO Coordinator,
Data General

(continued)

This is an invaluable tool for a company's self-appraisal. Effectively conducted, the results of an audit can lay a foundation for decision making toward the goal of improving operations.

DARYL PARKER,
Director, A.G.A. Quality,
ISO Registrar

The timing of an internal audit should be carefully planned and scheduled. An audit report should be written at the completion of the audit and distributed to the responsible departments for action. Other tips include:

- *Personnel can be brought in from different divisions and as many departments as possible.*

- *Auditor qualifications should be listed.*

- *Audit results should indicate that audit frequency is sufficient.*

- *Environmental auditing, should also be considered where appropriate.*

- *An outside organization can be used for internal auditing.*

- *Auditor checklists should periodically be reviewed and updated if necessary.*

ANDREW BERGMAN,
Manager of Certification,
OTS Quality Registrars

4.18

Training

If our people develop faster than a competitor's people, then they're worth more.

JIM BIGGAR, CEO,
Nestle Corporation

QUICK SCAN
ISO 9001 Requirements

Customer quality requirements are identified and internalized. Job specifications and procedures are spelled out so employees can perform the required work in a quality manner. Employee job skills, education, experience, and proficiency are periodically evaluated. Employees are trained and provided the resources they need in order to do their jobs. Training records are maintained and updated. Additional training is authorized when skills gaps are noticed.

THE BRAVE NEW WORKPLACE

Job homesteading is history. Companies are downsizing or outsourcing jobs. In the 1990s and beyond, Americans will have to develop a set of portable, marketable skills and migrate to jobs that afford the best opportunities. Many people will become migrant professionals, contractors, supervisors, or laborers.

What's required to survive and prosper in this economy? Global competitiveness will force people to become individually competitive—to develop a number of transferable and marketable skills. Loving change will be a mandate for job, family, health, and mental security. Career pundits already speculate that global changes will force people to have as many as six or more careers through their working lives.

TRAINING FOR COMPETITIVENESS

Large companies are pushing quality, cost, and technology requirements down the supplier chain. This can be seen as even small shops have to comply with quality standards, such as ISO 9000. Training is no longer considered a benefit for just a chosen few. It is a requirement for business survival. Often, all employees are provided one or two weeks of training a year in targeted skills or job training. New hires are extensively trained in the employer's quality systems, processes, and products.

Externally, the message to suppliers is "You must comply with our quality or technology requirements if you want to be on the approved bidder's list." The customer also tells the supplier, "We'll help you, but the responsibility to meet requirements is still yours." The only way to meet customer requirements is through improving operations. Suppliers—often small companies, which make up the bulk of U.S. employers—are sending the same message to their employees: "To earn you gotta learn."

Xerox was one of the first companies to recognize the importance of lifelong learning. In the late 1980s, Xerox was losing market share in the photocopier market to the Japanese. To reverse its fortune, Xerox trained all of its employees and many of its suppliers in quality principles and techniques. Two overarching objectives directed Xerox's quality training:

1. Customers must be satisfied every time.

2. Quality improvement is the responsibility of every employee.[1]

The effort resulted in dramatic increases in product quality, a 40 percent increase in customer satisfaction, and a 60 percent decrease in complaints.

Tips for Developing Effective Training Materials

Tips for developing company- and system-specific quality-training materials include:

- Base examples and case studies on the business.

- Base the assessment of specific training needs on job categories and existing skill levels.

- Design training to fit existing tools, techniques, and methods.

- Design training to fit the existing learning culture.

- Design the material to fit the management vision of quality improvement.

- Customize materials to fit the company.

- Include implementation, a tracking system, course evaluations, and feedback in the course schedule.

- Design course prerequisites and specific skills needed to make each module effective.

- Design exercises that contribute to an existing work situation.[2]

HOW MUCH TRAINING IS REQUIRED?

The number of initiatives promising competitiveness that have been introduced over the last several years is mind-boggling. Progressive organizations have implemented or are pursuing implementing just-in-time delivery, process reengineering, statistical process control, high-performance teams, cycle-time reduction, paperwork elimination, total customer service, and ISO certification.

What ties all these initiatives together is the need for continuous training. Each initiative requires employee knowledge and training on new systems, processes, procedures, and equipment.

Training is expensive. However, the cost of not training is even more expensive. It may mean the loss of business, reduced product quality, and increased exposure to risk. Hewlett-Packard employees receive more than 50 hours of work-related training per year, while IBM employees may receive as many as 80 hours. In smaller companies, depending on product lines and profitability, training can vary. The progressive view is that training is an investment in the future.

Specific training in quality-related technologies is found in most U.S. companies. Surveys indicate that more than 95 percent of U.S. companies have some in-house quality training for employees. More than 75 percent of the companies surveyed tend to concentrate training in three areas: production control, customer satisfaction, and supplier process control.[3]

TAILORED TRAINING

Training should be specific to a person's job and should emphasize measurable operational improvement. One reason for emphasizing this is because of the attention too often paid to the quick fix, used to get instant results. Quick fixes tend to promote

Learning How to Answer a Phone

An activity as simple as answering the phone has become an important element in the competitive struggle. Companies recognize that the phone is the first and maybe the last contact a customer may have with a company. First impressions developed over the phone tend to last. The telephone becomes the voice and image of a company.

Many companies have developed exhaustive training programs for their telephone representatives. Responsiveness and courtesy become two essential ingredients of the company's quality image for attracting and retaining customers. One organization has developed a five-step quality-improvement process for answering the telephone:

1. Plan for telephone quality.

2. Develop measurable performance standards and integrate them into the employee's job description and progress reviews.

3. Conduct telephone responsive training for all employees.

4. Reward and recognize employees who meet or exceed expectations.

5. Maintain a high level of telephone etiquette and awareness.[4]

quick solutions, scattered efforts, and false starts, but do not promote long-term improvement and sustained progress.

What proves that training works? Training works when employees have a definite stake in what is occurring in their workplace. Only then will people become excited about their work and commit to improving a company's processes and systems. ISO training also works if it is delivered in an informal setting in which everyone is involved. The goal is for employees to immediately put the learning into use in the workplace.[5] Customer service and management training illustrate the importance of the changes occurring in the workplace.

Customer Service Training

Customer service has become indispensable for all companies. Typically, customer service used to be an "afterthought" activity, peripheral to the main mission of the company. Companies now want to integrate the customer's voice throughout the organization and make it part of everyone's mission.

More companies are investing not just in satisfying customers but in developing exceptional customer service. Top companies, including L.L. Bean and Marriott, are empowering employees to solve customer problems immediately without having to secure management approval. L.L. Bean is committing the organization to total customer satisfaction. L.L. Bean has a no-questions-asked guarantee if a product is returned. Marriott also has been very successful by empowering its front-line service employees to immediately solve customer problems without securing management approval.[6] Federal Express trains all employees in a common quality language and ethos, and uses multidisciplinary teams to define problems, develop solutions, and continually improve upon the solutions.[7]

THE EXPERT'S CORNER
Insights and Tips

For us training is anything an employee is taught, even if an employee instructs another employee.
>   EMILY KONOLD,
>   Q.A. Specialist, Help/Systems

Although we had spent a good deal of time on training in the two years prior to the ISO effort, the training was reactive. It sprang from customer complaints or obvious system deficiencies and was always driven by the quality organization. By analyzing the system and using process improvement teams to study training issues, we began a systematic program of analysis based on both the needs of the organization and those of its members. This program has not only proven to be effective in creating an attitude of continuous improvement, but has instilled an attitude of continuous learning in the company.
>   JOHN ZAVACKI,
>   QA Manager, Suckle Corporation

We have found that grids and matrices are great to track who has been trained on what and to show training needs. Training is a key business need and requires management thought and shop-floor input. Documenting the processes wasn't as difficult as deciding what we really wanted and how to train personnel to reach that goal.
>   BETH KRENZER,
>   Manager, Black and White Film
>   Manufacturing, Eastman Kodak

Ensuring that employees are properly trained for the function performed has been key for our being able to provide quality products and services. Prior to the implementation of the ISO program, however, our process of maintaining training had been informal and inconsistent for most divisions. Constructing employees' training history records was difficult, particularly for those individuals who had been with the company for 15

(continued)

or more years. In some cases, the employee's training record only showed approximate dates.

The important element of the records is to confirm that the employee has received the minimum training required for the function performed, not necessarily all training the employee may have undergone. In our service division, a training database has been in place for many years for each field service engineer. Field engineers are trained in formal classroom settings for specific products. These training courses are also offered to our customers. The training database not only reflects the courses taken, but also the field engineer's efficiency level on a particular product.

> JOANNE MAYO,
> Corporate ISO Coordinator,
> Data General

The company should distinguish between training and indoctrination in their quality system. Indoctrination involves orienting personnel to the supplier's quality system, while training involves job-specific skills necessary for an individual to perform his or her job. Training should be department- or job-specific.

> ANDREW BERGMAN,
> Manager of Certification,
> OTS Quality Registrars

4.19

Servicing

High-quality service depends on high-quality management.
ROBERT E. KELLEY,
educator

QUICK SCAN
ISO 9001 Requirements

If the contract spells out service requirements, the following are general how-to-comply guidelines:

- Identify internal and external customer after-sales requirements.

- Plan after-sales activities.

- Verify design, maintenance, measurement, and test equipment used in after-sales service.

- Verify accuracy and completeness of documentation.

- Evaluate training and availability of personnel.

- Survey and verify that service level satisfies customers.

WHAT SEPARATES THE QUALITY WINNERS

As U.S. and Japanese auto quality converges, how do companies separate themselves from the competition? *Service.* Quality service on the ground, on the phone, and throughout the product's life distinguishes one quality product from another.

Products are a blend of tangible and intangible benefits. Both now have to be satisfied. Products are developed on the front end to be reliable and problem free. But if a product should fail, after-sales service fixes the problem in a courteous and reliable manner. This service is essential for guaranteeing continued customer satisfaction and building long-term loyalty.

The inspection and reaction mode of quality has changed to become preventive and preemptive, preventive in terms of eliminating product deficiencies from occurring or recurring, and preemptive in terms of anticipating customer requirements and being able to excel at satisfying them at each customer service point. After-sales service must be reliable and consistent. The quality of salespeople, facilities, delivery, and courtesy must be uniformly high.

Infiniti auto dealers are a success story and illustrate how to form close customer and supplier partnerships. When an Infiniti is brought in for a regular checkup, a loaner auto is supplied to the customer. When the customer picks up his or her car, it is cleaned inside and out and comes with a full tank of gas. This type of after-sales service builds customer loyalty and repeat sales. Infiniti knows this, having not just survived but prospered in the Japanese auto battles. Infiniti employees, including all its service advisers, are required to participate in a six-day training session at Infiniti University.[1]

AFTER-SALES SERVICE

For years, after-sales service meant having sufficient spare parts in case a product malfunctioned. This was part of the inspection and warranty mode of operation. A company knew whether it produced defective products, and the purpose of warranties was to ensure that the customer continued to be satisfied as problems arose. Products sometimes were designed, manufactured, and distributed with deficiencies in mind.

After-sales service provides unique positioning and advertising and selling potential. A company may offer trade-ins, guarantees, special services, promotional items, superior after-sales service, or any other inducements to promote customer loyalty. Companies have learned than it is much cheaper to retain a loyal customer than to find a new one.

The reliability of after-sales service is also important for the purchase of many products. Usually as products become more technical, after-sales service becomes more important. This is especially true with high-tech products. Once a person has been convinced to buy the high-tech product, he or she may have to be educated on how to use it.

THE EXPERT'S CORNER
Insights and Tips

The Field Service Organization had a sophisticated tracking system and technical support staff prior to the implementation of ISO. A toll free number provided customers with timely resolution of problems. Follow-up call placement confirmed complete customer satisfaction. Again, compliance to ISO was mainly documenting what was already performed.

In support of Field Service, the software organization provides customer service functions including training of field personnel prior to

(continued)

shipping a new revision of software, internships for systems engineers, and direct customer support, when required by the support center. Customer support representatives also participate in decisions to ship new revisions of software.

> JOANNE MAYO,
> Corporate ISO Coordinator,
> Data General

Procedures for servicing must be established. When servicing is included in the contract, provisions must be made to include this aspect in the quality system.

> ANDREW BERGMAN,
> Manager of Certification,
> OTS Quality Registrars

4.20

Statistical Techniques

When you are drowning in numbers you need a system to separate the wheat from the chaff.

ANTHONY ADAMS, V.P.,
Campbell Soup Company

QUICK SCAN
ISO 9001 Requirements

Statistical techniques are used to collect, analyze, and communicate information. Statistical methods can be used to analyze problems, determine risks, find root causes of a problem, verify results, establish process limits, or measure reliability. Most personnel should have at least a rudimentary knowledge of statistical analysis.

QUALITY TOOLS

Seven basic statistical quality tools are commonly used in manufacturing and service industries:

- Process-flow diagram.

- Cause-and-effect diagram.

- Pareto chart.

- Histogram.

- SPC chart.

- Trend chart.

- Scatter diagram.

These tools are often used in combination with one another. A process-flow diagram illustrates how a process works, which helps in understanding the nature of a problem. The cause-and-effect diagram identifies possible problems. These can be prioritized in a Pareto chart or a histogram. The Pareto chart may point out that 20 percent of the elements cause 80 percent or more of the problems. Statistical process control, trend, or scatter diagrams are used to understand and track variations in the process and to identify possible causes.

Business Examples

Statistics has broad uses in general and specific business applications:

GENERAL APPLICATIONS:

- Market/customer analysis.

- Product design.

- Process design.

- Project management.

- Team problem solving.

- Customer service.

- Risk analysis.

- Cause-and-effect diagrams.

STATISTICAL APPLICATIONS

- Process control/capability analyses.

- Sampling and inspection plans.

- Design of experiments.

- Reliability analysis.

- Cusum technique.

Statistical Process Control

Statistical process control (SPC) is probably the most commonly used statistical method. SPC is particularly used in the ongoing monitoring and measurement of a production system. Operators use the technique to understand how system variables can affect product quality. System variables may involve material hardness, methods to operate a machine, ambient conditions, or die wear. Each variable could alter the process, which would be indicated on the SPC chart.

In the last ten years, SPC has become more computer based. On-line computerized SPC includes automatic data collection, data analysis, identification of unusual conditions, and corrective action.[1]

THE EXPERT'S CORNER
Insights and Tips

We had to keep reminding ourselves that ISO 9002 doesn't state that you have to be doing SPC, but if you do have control charts, you had better be sure people are using them properly and have procedures to follow when charts indicate they are out of control. Don't forget that training records are very important.

> BETH KRENZER,
> Manager, Black and White Film
> Manufacturing, Eastman Kodak

Statistical techniques are utilized throughout the corporation to monitor and analyze product and process performance; therefore, documenting the methods used showed compliance with ISO requirements. In the manufacturing environment, statistical techniques are easy to conceptualize. In the service divisions, statistical tools were used (i.e., histograms, Pareto charts, etc.) but were not recognized as such until ISO implementation. In the design division, traditional quality management statistical tools are seldom used.

> JOANNE MAYO,
> Corporate ISO Coordinator,
> Data General

Appropriate statistical techniques are invaluable tools throughout the entire system. Properly utilized, they can assist in controlling processes and provide data that can be used as a basis for intelligent decision making.

> DARYL PARKER,
> Director, A.G.A. Quality,
> ISO Registrar

Statistical methods, when employed, shall be conducted according to established procedures. Statistical techniques are not ISO mandated and should be used where appropriate or at the discretion of the supplier.

ANDREW BERGMAN,
Manager of Certification,
OTS Quality Registrars

NOTES

Preface

1. ISO 9001, 4.4.2.2, Organizational and Technical Interfaces, 1987.

Chapter 1: Taking Care of Business

1. Myers, Ken. "Games Companies Play (and How to Stop Them)." *Training,* June 1992, pp. 68–70.
2. Hutchins, Greg. *Introduction to Quality: Management, Assurance, and Control,* Columbus, OH: Merrill/Macmillan, 1991, pp. 71–72.
3. J. Hagan. "The Management of Quality: Preparing for a Competitive Future." *Quality Progress,* November 1984, p. 12.

Chapter 2: What Are the ISO 9000 Standards?

1. Tattum, Lyn. "ISO 9000 in Europe: The Competitive Edge Is Dulled." *Chemical Week,* November 11, 1992.
2. Franklin, Barbara. "Quality and Competitiveness in a Changing World." *Business American,* October 19, 1992, pp. 35–37.
3. Weightman, R. T. "API and ISO Standards Can Be Combined." *Oil & Gas Journal,* November 16, 1992, pp. 50–52.
4. Plishner, Emily. "ISO 9000—Witco's Certification Plan: Total Immersion." *Chemical Week,* November 11, 1992, p. 54.
5. Plishner, Emily. "ISO 9000: Air Products: A Multisite Approach." *Chemical Week,* November 11, 1992, p. 56.

6. "Product Testing 'Most Valuable.' " *Quality in Manufacturing*, September/October 1993, p. 12.
7. Dillon, Tom. "Bogus Bolts Favor U.S. Producers." *Purchasing World*, August 1989, p. 50–51.

Chapter 3: Customer/Marketing Benefits

1. Tattum, Lyn. "ISO 9000 in Europe: The Competitive Edge Is Dulled." *Chemical Week*, November 11, 1992, pp. 37–38.
2. "Information Systems That Speed Product Delivery." *I/S Analyzer*, June 1990, pp. 1–12.

Chapter 4: Internal Benefits

1. Russell, J. P. "Six-Point Quality Planning." *Quality Progress*, pp. 55–58.
2. Dodson, Robert L. "Speeding the Way to Total Quality." *Training and Development*, June 1991, pp. 35–42.
3. Long, Ralph. "Protecting the Investment in People—Making Training Pay." *Journal of European Industrial Training*, 1990, pp. 21–27.
4. Holpp, Lawrence. "10 Reasons Why Total Quality Is Less than Total." *Training*, October 1989, pp. 93–103.

Chapter 5: Customer-Supplier Benefits

1. De Rose, Louis. "Industrial Buying Now Affected by Long-Term Strategy." *Marketing News*, May 28, 1990, p. 20.
2. Hutchins, Greg. *ISO 9000*. Essex Junction, VT: Oliver Wight Publishing, 1993, p. 32.
3. Witt, Clyde. "Partnership Drives Allison's Focused Factory." *Material Handling Engineering*, January 1992, pp. 36–40.
4. "Buyers Are Putting Guts into Supplier Rating Programs." *Purchasing*, March 9, 1989, pp. 24–26.
5. Wheatley, Malcolm. "Seattle Superstar." *Management Today*, December 1991, pp. 44–48.
6. Johnson, Elmer. "Phillips Plastics Achieves Total Quality Success." *Quality*, March 1991, pp. 22–24.

Chapter 6: Getting Started

1. Edosomwan, J. "Implementation Strategies for Quality Programs." *Industrial Engineering*, October 1992, p. 24.

2. Koger, Dan. "If Total Quality Seems Like a Revolution, That's Because It Is." *Communication World*, October 1992, pp. 18–21.

4.1 Management Responsibility

1. Ginnodo, William. "How TQM Is Redefining Management and Leadership." *Tapping the Network Journal*, Fall 1992, pp. 8–10.
2. Van Nuland, Yves. "Prerequisites to Implementation." *Quality Progress*, June 1990, pp. 36–39.

4.2 Quality Systems

1. "Quality Management and Quality Assurance Vocabulary." ASQ in Milwaukee, WI, 1991, p. 17.

4.3 Contract Review

1. Benson, Tracy. "World Class Organizations: Beyond Niche Marketing." *Industry Week*, September 17, 1990, pp. 12–19.

4.4 Design Control

1. Moon, Earl. "MRB Transition to Design Review." *Printed Circuit Design*, September 1991, pp. 24–28.

4.5 Document Control

1. Sanders, Robert. "Configuration Management's Concept of the Living Lessons for Records Management." *Records Management Quarterly*, October 1992, pp. 46–51.

4.8 Product Identification and Traceability

1. Caplan, Frank. Radnor, PA: Chilton Quality Systems, 1991.

4.10 Inspection and Testing

1. Phillip. "Using Machine Vision to Improve Quality and Process Control." *Modern Plastics*, July 1992, pp. 56–57.
2. Noaker, Paula. "Inspection/Quality Assurance." *Manufacturing Engineering*, August 1992, pp. 210–12.

4.11 Inspection, Measuring, and Test Equipment

1. Heller, Karen. "Compliance Benefits Staff at Ethyl: Understanding of Operations Is Enhanced." *Chemical Week*, April 29, 1992, p. 52.

4.13 Control of Nonconforming Product

1. Drori, Neil. "Taking the Bull Out of Bar Codes." *Bobbin*, February 1992, pp. 14–18.

4.14 Corrective Action

1. Teresko, John. "America's Best Plants: Nippondenso." *Industry Week*, October 21, 1991, pp. 47–48.
2. Webb, David. "The Point Is to Keep the Customer from Becoming Unhappy." *Electronic Business*, October 1992, pp. 115–16.
3. Blaisdell, Kenneth. "How Failure Analysis Fails." *Machine Design*, May 11, 1989, pp. 146–50.
4. Erin, Tim. "Closed-Loop Corrective Action." *Quality Progress*, January 1993, pp. 51–53.

4.15 Handling, Storage, Packaging, and Delivery

1. Woods, Douglas. "Innovative Partnership Programs." *Quality*, September 1992, pp. 23–24.
2. Harari, Oren. "Quality Is a Good Bit-Box." *Management Review*, December 1992, p. 8–9.
3. Ammons, James. "Small-Product Storage Options." *Plant Engineering*, June 22, 1989, pp. 69–70.
4. Larson, Melissa. "Labeler Speeds: How High Can They Go?" *Packaging*, May 1990, pp. 56–58.

4.16 Quality Records

1. Nearing, David. "Worth a Thousand Words." *Manufacturing Systems*, September 1991, pp. 50–51.

4.17 Internal Quality Audits

1. ANSI/ASQC Standard Q1—1986 Generic Guidelines for Auditing of Quality Systems, New York.
2. Blue, Lohman. "What Drives Quality?" *Internal Auditor*, April 1992, pp. 38–45.
3. Hutchins, Greg. *Quality Auditing*. New York: Prentice Hall Press, 1992, p. 54.

4.18 Training

1. Caudron, Shari. "How Xerox Won the Baldrige." *Personnel Journal*, April 1991, pp. 98–102.
2. Miller, John. "Training Required to Support Total Quality Management." *CMA Magazine*, November 1992, p. 29.
3. Morgan, James. "Quality: Up and Running." *Purchasing*, January, 16, 1992, pp. 69–71.
4. Chevalier, Mary. "Don't Just Answer the Phone—Use It." *Quality Progress*, June 1989, pp. 56–59.
5. Johnson, John. "The Problem with TQM Education." *Tapping the Network Journal*, Spring 1992, pp. 21–23.
6. Penzer, Erika. "Is the Customer Always Right?" *Incentive*, May 1990, pp. 22–36.
7. Keeter, Margaret. "Quality Training." *Training Magazine*, March 1991, pp. 15–25.

4.19 Servicing

1. Barrett, Amy. "After-Sales Service: Infiniti." *Financial World*, April 14, 1992, p. 49.

4.20 Statistical Techniques

1. Scott, Steven. "A Three-Phase Model for Quality." *Quality*, June 6, 1991, Q2–Q4.

GLOSSARY

Accreditation: Procedures by which an authoritative body recognizes the ability of a group to conduct registration activities or tests.

ASQC: Acronym for American Society for Quality Control.

Auditee: Organization or area being audited.

Auditor: Person qualified to conduct quality audits.

CAR: Acronym for Corrective Action Request.

Closed correction action loop: Process steps ensuring that problems don't recur.

Conformity: Ability to satisfy requirements.

Contract review: Analysis by supplier to determine ability to satisfy customer's requirements.

Contractor: Provider of products or services to customer; same as supplier.

Control: Compare against standard; to exercise authority over.

Corrective action: Actions to eliminate the symptom and the root cause of a nonconformance.

Customer: Recipient of products or services from supplier.

Defect: Same as nonconformity.

Deficiency: Not fulfilling or satisfying a customer's requirements.

Final inspection: Test of the overall product's performance, appearance, reliability, or serviceability.

Incoming inspection: A visual or a dimensional check of quality attributes of incoming materials from external or internal suppliers.

In-process inspection: Assessment of product quality attributes as they are being produced or machined.

Inspection: Method of evaluating conformity to requirements by testing, measuring, or observing.

Nonconformity: State of not satisfying requirements.

Organization: Company or group of people performing defined activities.

Partnering: Alliance between or among parties to share ideas, resources, designs, and other capabilities for improving one's competitiveness.

Prevention: Actions to deter problems or deficiencies from occurring or recurring.

Procedure: Set of defined and/or documented activities or actions.

Process: Actions transform inputs into outputs; preferably process adds value to inputs.

Product: Output of a process; can be tangible or intangible service.

Purchaser: Buyer of products or services; also called the customer.

Qualification process: Process of determining ability of supplier or other party to satisfy requirements; also called certification process.

Qualified: Demonstrating ability to satisfy requirements; same as certified.

Quality: Ability to satisfy the customer; characteristic of a product relating to its ability to satisfy the customer.

Quality assurance: Planned and systematic quality system activities to ensure that quality requirements are met.

Quality audit: Systematic, objective, and independent evaluation of quality plan.

Quality control: Operational monitoring and supervision to ensure that quality requirements are met.

Quality improvement: Actions to increase efficiency, effectiveness, and economy of organizational area.

Quality loop: Model of process steps from identifying requirements to satisfying them.

Quality manual: Company documents listing quality and operational policies.

Quality plan: Quality document describing activities, resources, and sequence of operations to attain product quality; quality systems and other activities; sometimes called quality assessment.

Quality requirements: Customer criteria found in rules, codes, regulations, specifications, and drawings.

Quality system: Required processes, procedures, structure to implement Total Quality Management.

Rework: Work on nonconforming products to verify that they conform to requirements.

Sampling: Probability-based technique used to indicate the number of products to be pulled from a lot or batch for inspection.

Service: Intangible product provided by a supplier.

SPC: Acronym for Statistical Process Control; statistical method for monitoring, correcting, and improving processes.

Specification: Documents stating requirements.

Subcontractor: Provider of products or services to contractor; same as supplier's supplier.

Supplier: Provider of products or services to customer.

Traceability: Ability to trace history and location of a product through production, design, or other process.

INDEX